MASON∗DIXON
KNITTING

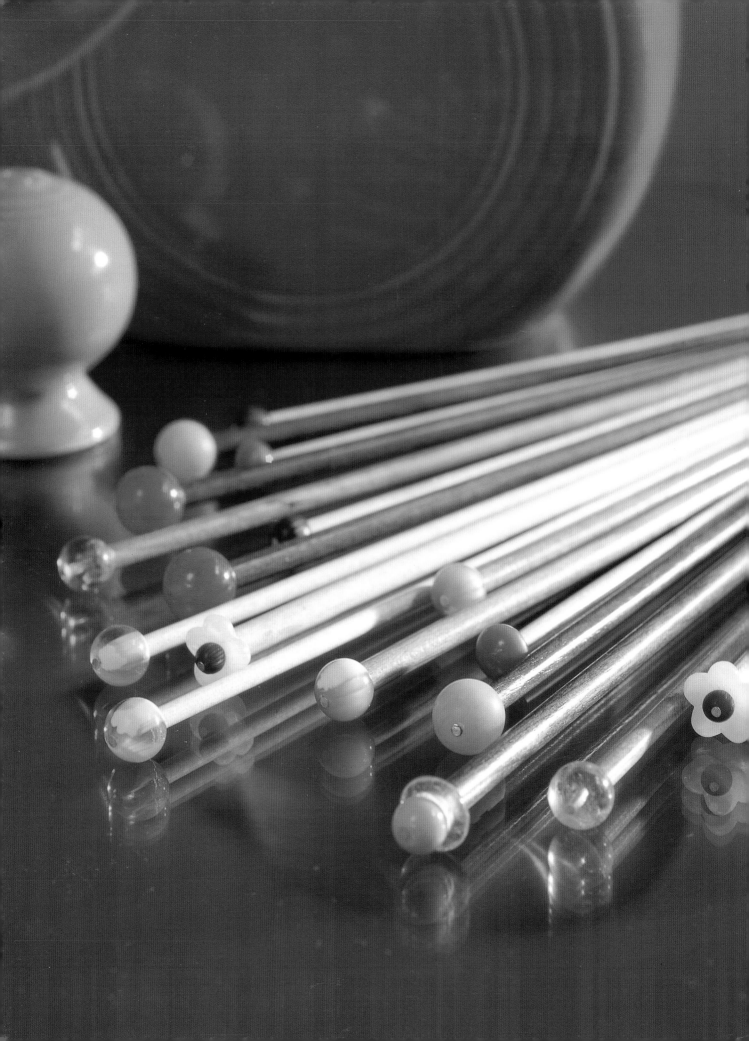

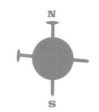

MASON*DIXON KNITTING

★ ★

THE CURIOUS KNITTERS' GUIDE

STORIES, PATTERNS, ADVICE,
OPINIONS, QUESTIONS, ANSWERS, JOKES, AND PICTURES

★ ★

Kay Gardiner and Ann Shayne

PHOTOGRAPHS BY STEVE GROSS AND SUE DALEY

POTTER
CRAFT

NEW YORK

Copyright © 2006 by Kay Gardiner and Ann Shayne
Photographs copyright © 2006 by Steve Gross and Sue Daley
All rights reserved.

Published in the United States by Potter Craft,
an imprint of the Crown Publishing Group,
a division of Random House, Inc., New York.

www.crownpublishing.com
www.pottercraft.com

POTTER CRAFT and colophon is a
registered trademark of Random House, Inc.

Originally published in hardcover in the United States by
Potter Craft, an imprint of the Crown Publishing Group,
a division of Random House, Inc., New York, in 2006.

Library of Congress Cataloging-in-Publication Data
is available upon request.

ISBN: 978-0-307-58645-2

Printed in Singapore

Design by Chalkley Calderwood Pratt

Illustration on cover and on p.9 copyright © 2006 by
Agnes Barton-Sabo of Hatch Show Print

10 9 8 7 6 5 4 3 2 1

First Paperback Edition

For
our families:

Hubby,
Carrie,
and Joseph
★
Hubbo,
David,
and Clifton

* CONTENTS *

A FANTASTIC VOYAGE BEGINS

From: Ann Shayne
Date: Fri May 24, 2002 9:59:20 AM
Subject: cheers!

Hello Kay!

Polly posted an update about your daughter Carrie, and I was so sorry to hear you'd been in the thick of it. I asked Polly for your e-mail address, which she obviously passed along. (I hope that was OK.)

Just wanted you to know that there are thoughts and prayers coming your way for a speedy recovery. We'll all look forward to having you back in the forum when Carrie is all better.

Every best wish,
Ann

From: Kay Gardiner
Date: Thu May 30, 2002 5:41:16 PM
Subject: Re: cheers!

Thanks Ann! I am feeling SO MUCH better this week because Carrie is much better and we are assured that her illness was really a freakish thing that is not likely to repeat itself.

Whodathunkit—that one's knitting chat-site could be such a mainstay! But it is. I feel lucky to have tapped into it before all this happened and can't wait to get back on and catch up on the zany sock-knitters, et al. Thanks so much for the thoughts and prayers.

Love,
Kay

Ann

Thoughts and prayers. For a sick girl I'd never met, whose mother I'd never met. *Thoughts and prayers?* What is up with that? I'm not a thoughts-and-prayers-sending kind of person. But there I was, worried about this woman and her daughter.

It's not like we were best pals or anything. Kay and I had been yakking online for a couple of months at the Rowan Yarns online forum, shooting the breeze about the burning issues of the day: sleeves that were too long, the merits of Summer Tweed yarn. I knew that she lived in New York, and that she had at some point run a marathon. But that was it. She was mad for Rowan's yarns, and so was I. That was plenty. Neither of us had ever corresponded with anybody online, but we were having a fine old time hanging out with all those British knitters whose slang was a constant education to us. When Kay disappeared from the forum, I wondered what had happened. When I learned from our fellow Rowanette Polly that Kay's daughter was very sick, I felt a lurch. Must send thoughts and prayers. Quick: Get the thoughts and prayers activated.

THE MASON-DIXON
MANIFESTO
• PEACE
• LOVE
• NATURAL FIBERS
(not necessarily in
that order)

When Kay wrote back to me about her daughter's unexpected, terrifying illness, I instantly wrote back about my own brush with sick family. Just like that, I let it fly. We moved through the perils of staying home with children after loving your career (How not to feel like a free-loader? It's impossible!), the merits of Jackson Browne (Kay stands firm; I waver), and the large and prickly topic of marriage. (When your husband leaves three months' worth of *Barron's* on the floor, can you throw it out?) We found endless things in common—Jewish husbands, our own un-Jewishness, two kids, fast typing, encyclopedic knowledge of Patsy Cline lyrics, a morbid fear of things that smell bad. We weren't Internet pals, we were freaky Internet twins. It seemed antique to have a correspondent, even if the correspondent was corresponding on a computer hooked up to the Internet. At many moments I felt like picking up the phone, but I feared the spell would break and the midwestern-born Kay would sound like some character from *Fargo,* or she would discover just how superfakeynice I really am.

Our Thelma-and-Louise-drive-the-car-over-the-cliff moment of true friendship came after about a year of e-mails. Shameless eBay hounds, we both noticed a sizable lot of old

Never has a felted chair seat cover been attempted with such fervor.

knitting books up for auction. It was the Mother Lode, the last great undisturbed stash of Rowanalia, being deaccessioned by an actual lady in Yorkshire, the home turf of Rowan Yarns—the provenance, the provenance! Picasso's sketchbooks turning up on eBay would not have caused a greater frenzy. Even for us, with our skewed financial orientation (in which the eBay yarn tab took priority over the light bill), it was a stretch to think that we had to possess these books. And that we would throw in our lot together to buy this huge pile of possibly moldy old stuff that potentially could smell bad, well. . . . It was a pinky promise commitment.

Fifty pounds of knitting books. So glad Hubbo never saw this.

I watched the final moments of the auction tick away, waiting for eSnipe to make our sneak-attack bid, and we won. The phone rang. Yikes! I just about jumped out of my skin. "Rilly? It's *you*?" I said, sounding stupid. What's funny is that I had had the same impulse to call her to mark this ridiculous moment. Kay was glad I didn't sound like a character on *The Dukes of Hazzard* as she had feared. I was relieved that she didn't say *okeydokey*. We hung up, then headed off to fork over the PayPal payment of the year. In a couple of weeks, fifty pounds of old magazines landed at my house.

In the course of our copious correspondence, we critiqued knitting books, patterns, magazines. Between the two of us, we owned probably 90 percent of the knitting books in print—hell, we had *Knitted Clowns*. It was our little obsession, which we wedged into the crevices of free time that motherhood allowed. Some people collect glass Christmas ornaments or rubber stamps; we had our books.

All the while we were knitting, knitting, *knitting*. Those books—which did not smell bad, after all our worrying—were a PhD program in pattern-making, technique, and style, filled with lessons about why the '80s are best left unrevisited. We took our endless e-mails onto the Internet with a weblog, Mason-Dixon Knitting. We absorbed our readers' wisdom and wackiness with glee. Such a group! We began to branch out, to experiment, inspired by the people we were meeting. This knitting thing. . . . It began to seem so rich: with ideas, with friends, with the potential for anything.

One morning in the kitchen, Clifton, my then four-year-old son, was practicing his Buzz Lightyear imitation, flailing around with an Eggo waffle as his weapon. As the maple syrup made spin art all over the furniture, I wished my chairs had protection. I conjured up a project that had no pattern, that was something I wanted but didn't quite know how to make. For the first time in my knitting career, I was going to wing it. I . . . was . . . *free*.

It doesn't sound all that revolutionary, the notion that you can concoct an idea for something, especially something as clear cut as a felted chair seat cover. But for Kay and me, knitting began as the paint-by-numbers process of following a pattern. Believe me: There is a time and a place for the comfort of a beautiful pattern, well written and tidy. But we have come to discover that a pattern can be a starting line, a launching pad. Who knows what's going to happen? The possibility of ending up with a handknit that has the mark of your own imagination on it is a powerful and delicious thing.

Kay

WHAT YOU WILL LEARN FROM THIS BOOK

Mason-Dixon
Rule Number 462:
WING IT!

We have discovered wondrous creations in our road trip through Knitopia. Pillows with fingerprints knitted on them. Seven-foot-high crocheted tents. A portrait of Virginia Woolf, knitted. The maze at Chartres cathedral, knitted. Crocheted vines wandering up a German lamppost. The flat-out whimsy and genius in these epic projects leaves us blinking our eyes in astonishment.

We plan at some point to make log cabin blankets that re-create our Easter photos circa 1967. We got this idea after seeing *Unexpected Knitting* (Schoolhouse Press, 2003), in which Debbie New shows a bedspread-sized portrait of her grandmother. It is the most spectacular project we have ever seen. Yet as stunning as it is, the blanket is made of log cabin squares. A simple technique. Over and over, we see this same phenomenon: complex things are often very simple.

And simple things can be very beautiful. There are thirty-four patterns in this book, most of which are the epitome of ease. You can make 'em easy, or you can make 'em as complicated as you can bear. The intention here is to leave room for you to expand on what we have been exploring ourselves. We show you how to make a log cabin blanket; if you have a family photo that you want to recapture in eight-by-ten-foot glory, by golly, you'll leave this book with the necessary skill set.

We delight in introducing you to extraordinary people we have met whose open-minded knitting has inspired us. Their projects are included here, because they show you a cool idea, and leave room for you to make it your own.

It is possible to fill a cedar chest with perfect replicas of every single item in this book. But we hope that by the time you have read through *Mason-Dixon Knitting*, you'll take these ideas and run with them. Look around your own life. Your own experiences, surroundings, and family are chock full of potential. Surely you have a surface in your home that has not yet been covered in the appropriate handknit. Surely you have some ancestor, a tidy aunt or a grandmotherly grandmother, who has left behind a legacy you can draw from. Ann sees Grommy's needlepoint chair, and she ends up with a knitted piano bench cushion. I attend an exhibit at the Whitney Museum of American Art, and find myself with a blanket based on a quilt I admired on the gallery wall.

Incredible as it may seem, we are eager to play with these patterns more, even though we have been living with them for months now. Remember: knitting and life intersect. Figuring out how you can knit the two together? That's the fun part.

So, come have a seat, and bring out your knitting. We have lots to show you.

Before long, you'll
find bags filled with
knitting on every
doorknob.

Chapter One

BEING*A*BEGINNER

I AM THINKING BACK TO THE DAYS when I first learned **TO*KNIT.** I was knitting too much, **BUT EVEN A CRIPPLED ELBOW** wouldn't stop me. **KNIT THROUGH THE PAIN.** Must keep knitting!

Ann ✳ Last week five-year-old Clif asked me what was the hardest thing I'd ever done. When I started to answer, "Getting you into preschool," I realized that he was talking heaviest object lifted or tallest mountain climbed. I told him I once did a back flip on a trampoline and it scared me half to death.

"Wow," he said. "That's dangerous."

"Yes indeedy."

Knitting definitely did not come to mind. But I am thinking back to the days when I first learned to knit. Oh, the difficulty! I got that crampy shoulder feeling, and this one ropey thing in my right arm hurt like crazy. I was knitting too much, but even a crippled elbow wouldn't stop me. Knit . . . through . . . the pain . . . . Must . . . keep . . . knitting . . . .

The agony of knitting beat the daily grind of my job at a publishing house in Manhattan. Knitting was the perfect antidote to a job filled with endless piles of manuscripts that would never be published yet had to be read, or at least stared at, by me. Knitting was nonverbal. It had a beginning, a middle, and an end. The problems of knitting were solvable: the worst thing that could happen was that I had to rip something out. Mistakes would disappear, just like that. I would complete something.

I still have the first sweater I made. Holy muddah of God, it's a hot item: a wool and silk blend, knitted on at least size 11 needles, two rectangles and two trapezoids sewn together using the um-whatever method of seaming. It isn't much, and I've hardly ever worn it because the temperature rarely drops below zero here in Nashville. But here's the thing: I made that sweater in 1987, and I've never gotten rid of it. I was so proud to have created something of my own that I have kept it, a tender memento of a particular place and time.

WHERE TO BEGIN

If possible, get someone you love to teach you to knit. In 1987, I was working in New York, far from my homeland of Dixie. I didn't have a fluffy-haired grandmother at hand, so I took a class at the Learning Annex. (It was either knitting or "How to Receive Messages from the Beyond.") This was in the dark ages of knitting, before adorable shops with yarn-upholstered walls beckoned. I learned to cast on in a public school classroom on Manhattan's East Side, bleak and unwelcoming but proof that when knitting grips you, you'll knit anywhere.

I envy women who learned to knit from their mother or aunt or next-door neighbor. If you're lacking a mother or aunt or next-door neighbor, borrow one. Ideally she should be at least twenty years older than you, and at some point have had a deep involvement with Red Heart acrylic yarn. Knitting is one of the best ways young folks and old folks can spend time together, and if you're on the younger side, learning to knit is an opportunity to hear stories that you otherwise would miss. If you're on the older side, knitting is your ticket to a wondrous place called Youth. You will be amazed at how different, and how identical, the concerns of the youngsters are to yours. You can be of help.

When you've located your knitting mentor, head for the nearest yarn store. Take a deep breath when you discover what a ball of yarn can cost. But even a giant hank of the priciest handpaint is quite a bit less than most psychotherapy sessions, and the fact is that the time you spend with that yarn may well be more therapeutic than an hour of the talking cure. Go ahead and buy great yarn. Don't think it's not worth it to use the good stuff because you're just starting out. Good yarn holds up, feels great, has prettier colors, and is a lovely gift to yourself. After all, who's more deserving than *you*? As our friend Jill Richards puts it, "I never regret my luxuries; only my economies."

If you're reading this, you have probably already made something. It's likely that you have made a scarf, or at least part of one. We're not big fans of the scarf as a first project: The insane euphoria of starting out tends to bog down once you start to get the hang of it, and the demoralizing second half of a scarf can suck the joy out of the whole idea.

But finishing a scarf, well. The satisfaction of wearing a handmade object of your own making is intoxicating. More, more, more! Bring on the handknits!

GREAT THINGS YOU WILL DO
★ ★ ★ ★ ★ ★ ★ ★ ★

YOU WILL...
knit far into the night.

YOU WILL...
wake up and start knitting before you've had any coffee.

YOU WILL...
buy more yarn before you have finished your first project.

YOU WILL...
buy a pattern book.

YOU WILL...
Google "yarn."

YOU WILL...
finish something and feel like you've reached the top of Mount Kilimanjaro.

If the Anti-Dishcloth
Coalition targets you for
making dishcloths, resist
peacefully and start
singing Bob Dylan songs.

IN DEFENSE OF THE WARSHRAG

We're all for recycling and going organic and running vehicles on leftover french fry oil. (OK, we love a leather shoe and you can't take that away from us.) But even as a knitted dishcloth is a reusable resource that has the potential to shut down the paper towel industry, we like it because it's fun. When you knit a dishcloth, you are making something you will use every day. It gives you endless opportunity to mess around with stitch patterns. And after you have made a bunch of them, you'll be greeted by a drawer full of shiny sunshine every time you go to mop up a river of maple syrup. Despite being the simplest thing in the world to make, a knitted dishcloth is something you can give your sister with a deluxe cake of soap, give to

You'll consider selling your old *dishcloths* on eBay...

a new mom with some of that organic baby shampoo made from slippery bark, or send to a faraway friend for a housewarming present.

If you're making a dishcloth, it needs to be cotton. There is no more perfect choice than Peaches & Creme, a cotton yarn made by the good people of Elmore-Pisgah Incorporated. We like chatting with the friendly folks who answer the phone there in Spindale, North Carolina. Unlike many yarns, Peaches & Creme is so reasonably priced that you can buy a cone of it—840 glorious yards, enough for a pile of dishcloths—for the same price as a movie ticket. It tightens up with washing, the colors fade, and before long you have something that for all the world looks like it came from 1933. You'll consider selling your old dishcloths on eBay, they're so vintagey.

The other virtue of making dishcloths early in your knitting career is that it cures you of the dreaded disease known as Precious Knits Syndrome. I suffered from this for years: If it was knitted by my hands, it was treasure, never to be thrown away or even washed very much. I still have every single swatch I ever made—I'm the one with that unwearable sweater from 1987, remember? It is true that something you make yourself is a very special thing. We will be writing later about heirlooms and things that need to be wrapped in acid-free tissue and tenderly placed on a clean shelf for descendants to discover a hundred years from now. But how cool is it to make something that has an actual function in your life! It's how knitting started, all those centuries ago: Somebody got chilly, decided to go online and order some yarn, and voilà—a craft was born.

The classic slip-stitch dishcloth has been around since the time of Beowulf. It's such a perennial favorite that it's reprinted on the Peaches & Creme label. We include it here because, when you're done with it, you've accomplished several things at once: It shows you what happens when you slip a stitch. It allows you to use more than one color of yarn. And it ends up looking all complicated, and who doesn't want to look like a genius?

A TIMELINE OF KNITTING HISTORY

1595 B.C.:
Woman waiting for Hittite husband to return from sacking of Babylon picks up string and two sticks, begins "Support Our Troops" scarf.

1595 B.C.
(two minutes later): Woman drops first stitch, utters first curse word related to knitting.

A.D. 1215:
Woman waiting in lobby for husband to finish reading the Magna Carta picks up string and piece of wire left over from husband's armor; invents the fishing gansey.

A.D. 1215
(ten minutes later): Husband comes out, says, "What are you doing, milady?" Woman says, "Shut up, I'm counting."

1346:
Knitting guilds form. From the charter: "For the attainement of wages and goode skilles. If ye be a male, and ye knit, ye shalle joinne. If ye be a female, buzze offe."

1620:
Pilgrim ladies plan knitting circle, discover lack of yarn shops in the New World, take up decorative shoe buckle-making instead.

BALLBAND DISHCLOTH

Here's the classic dishcloth recipe that goes with Peaches & Creme the way champagne goes with truffles. Or a Diet Rite Cola with a Moon Pie, to be more exact.

SIZE: Approx 9¼" x 9¼" (23.5 cm x 23.5 cm)

MATERIALS: Peaches & Creme worsted weight by Elmore-Pisgah Inc., [solid colors 2½ oz (71.5 g) balls, each approx 122yds (112 m); ombre colors 2 oz (57 g) balls, each approx 98 yds (90 m), cotton] 1 ball each in color A and color B
Size 7 (4.5 mm) needles

GAUGE: 18 sts + 32 rows = 4" (10 cm) over pat st.

With A, CO 45 sts (loosely).

ROW 1: Using A, knit.

ROW 2: Purl.

ROW 3: Join B, k4, slip 1 purlwise *k5, sl 1 purlwise; rep from * to last 4 sts, k4.

ROW 4: K4, yarn forward (yf), slip 1 purlwise, yarn back (yb), *k5, yf, slip 1 purlwise, yb; rep from * to last 4 sts, k4.

ROW 5: P4, yb, slip 1 purlwise, yf, *p5, yb, slip 1 purlwise, yf; rep from * to last 4 sts, p4.

ROW 6: Repeat Row 4.

ROW 7: Using A, knit.

A dishcloth ain't a dishcloth until it has been used on a dish. Must. Use. The. Handknits.

ROW 8: Purl.

ROW 9: Using B, k1, slip 1 purlwise, *k5, slip 1 purlwise; rep from * to last st, k1.

ROW 10: K1, yf, slip 1 purlwise, yb, *k5, yf, slip 1 purlwise, yb; rep from * to last st, k1.

ROW 11: P1, yb, slip 1 purlwise, yf, *p5, yb, slip 1 purlwise, yf; rep from * to last st, p1.

ROW 12: Repeat Row 10.

Repeat these 12 rows 5 times, then rep rows 1 through 8. BO loosely.

Remember to take off your apron and hairnet before leaving the house.

1793:
Eli Whitney invents the cotton gin.

1896:
Siobahn Ogwnngyfleioghnn knits so poorly that she accidentally discovers the cable stitch.

1924:
Kleenex invented.

1924
(one hour later): Mildred Farnwinkle of Dubuque, Iowa, completes first Kleenex box cozy.

1968:
Janis Joplin wears crochet vest at Woodstock. Jimi Hendrix is heard to say, "Nice vest, Janis. I love that colorway."

1997:
Eyelash yarn invented. On the Isle of Lewis, Alice Starmore weeps into her twenty-eight-shade Fair Isle sleeve.

Kay

HEARTBREAKINGLY CUTE BABY KIMONO

All you need to know when you start out is how to (1) cast on, (2) knit (purling is for show-offs), and (3) bind off. This one-piece baby kimono is an ideal project for a beginner, because in the course of the project, you will learn how to do a make one (M1) or yarn over (yo) increase. This will make you feel like an expert if it's new to you.

Even if you're not a beginner, it's fun to construct an entire garment in a single piece. Only two seams to sew, and it's done.

And did we mention that it's *cheap*? People are always saying that it doesn't matter how much a gift costs, but this is one of the rare instances in which that is actually true. We used Peaches & Creme cotton. Two balls. It will cost you more to wrap it. Yet there couldn't be a cuter, or more tender, gift to welcome a newborn.

This pattern was designed by the redoubtable Cristina Shiffman, a talented reader of our blog. She mentioned that she had come up with a tiny kimono in dishcloth cotton. We always perk up our ears at the words *dishcloth cotton*. Tell us more, we said.

We get a special thrill out of making something so perfect and elegant out of humble dishcloth cotton. But this tiny garment is a lily that you can gild as much or as little as you like. If you feel a strong urge to spend a bit more dough and make this little wrapper in cashmere, linen, or mercerized cotton, go ahead. So little yarn is required that you cannot break the bank, try as you might.

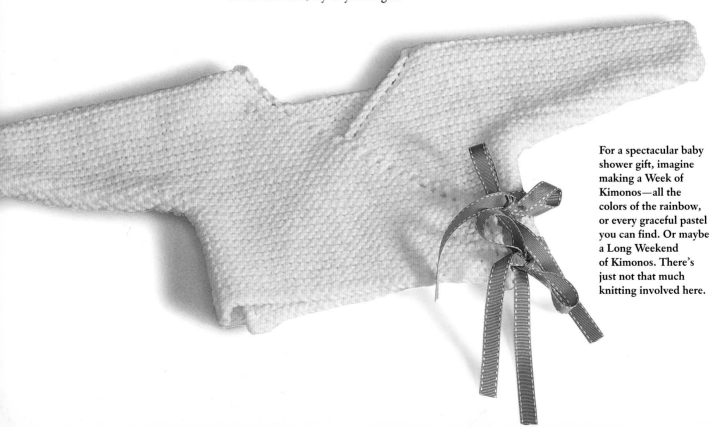

For a spectacular baby shower gift, imagine making a Week of Kimonos—all the colors of the rainbow, or every graceful pastel you can find. Or maybe a Long Weekend of Kimonos. There's just not that much knitting involved here.

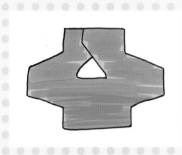

ONE-PIECE BABY KIMONO

By Cristina Shiffman

Cristina's lovely annotated sketch of this kimono pattern looked like a map from *Raiders of the Lost Ark*. I puzzled and thought there was no way I could figure it out. But once I put the needles in my hands and cast on 40 stitches, I was off to the races. Cristina was right! It *is* easy as pie!

The instructions are the same regardless of whether you use garter stitch or stockinette.

SIZE: Newborn. (You can easily enlarge it by casting on more stitches and adding rows to the body and sleeves.)

MATERIALS: Peaches & Creme worsted weight by Elmore-Pisgah Inc., [solid colors 2½ oz (71.5 g) balls, each approx 122yds (112m)]; 2 balls in white
Size 6 (4 mm) needles or size needed to achieve gauge
½" grosgrain ribbon, 1yd (1 m)

GAUGE: 20 sts + 40 rows = 4" (10 cm) over garter st.

Body

CO 40 sts. Working in either garter stitch or stockinette stitch, work for 4" (10 cm), ending with a WS row.

Using the "thumb" or "backward loop" cast-on method, CO 3 stitches at the beginning of each of the next 16 rows, ending with a WS row (88 sts). The newly cast-on stitches form the sleeves.

Work even for 6 rows.

NEXT ROW (RS): K34, BO center 20 sts, k to end of row. (You will now be working the left sleeve and the left front of the kimono. Instructions for finishing the right side follow.)

On the next and every following RS row, inc 1 st at neck edge, using either the yarn over or make one increase.

Vive la Différence

What is the difference between the two methods? In the "Yarn Over" (YO) method, the increase forms a decorative hole, or eyelet. The "Make One" (M1) increase, while detectable, is less obvious. The choice is a matter of which look you prefer.

Continue until the sleeve is 4" (10 cm) wide at the wrist. BO 3 sts at the beginning of the next 8 WS rows. AT THE SAME TIME, continue to inc 1 stitch at the neck edge on every RS row in the same manner (see diagram).

Continue until the left front is 40 stitches, and until, when the sleeve is folded in half, the kimono front is the same length as the back. BO all stitches.

Rejoin yarn to the sts of the right sleeve at the neck edge (WS). Work to the end of the row. On the next and every following RS row, inc 1 st at neck edge, using the same method as you used on the other front edge.

Continue in this manner until the sleeve is 4" (10 cm) wide at the wrist. BO 3 sts at the beginning of the next 8 RS rows. AT THE SAME TIME, continue to inc 1 st at the neck edge on every RS row in the same manner.

Continue until the right front is 40 sts wide. Work even until the right front has the same number of rows as the left front. BO all stitches.

Finishing

Sew in all ends on the WS. Dampen the kimono and, with WS facing, lay it on a towel on a smooth surface. Shape with your fingers, straightening the edges. Let it dry.

Sew the underarm and sleeve seams using mattress stitch. Sew 9" (23 cm) lengths of ribbon into the left side seam, placing them 1" (2.5 cm) apart. Line up the right front overlapping the left front, and sew two ribbons onto the edge of the right front, opposite the ribbons in the left seam.

TECHNICAL HINTS

How to Do a Make One Increase ★ One stitch in from the edge, use the needle tip to lift the horizontal strand that lies between the stitch you have just completed and the next stitch. Place the stitch onto the left needle. Then knit it through the back of the loop.

How to Do a Yarn Over Increase ★ On a RS knit row, bring the yarn in front as if you were going to purl the next stitch. Instead, insert your right needle into the next stitch as if to knit and knit the stitch, bringing the yarn back around the right needle as when knitting normally. On the next row, when you get to the place where you brought the yarn in front on the previous row, you will see an extra loop. Work this loop, also known as a "yarn over," as if it were a regular stitch.

Remember: Linen is the yarn of the gods—the gods who know that even if a yarn is a little starchy to knit, it's worth it because it will soften, relax, and last through the apocalypse.

Ann

PRISS UP YOUR POWDER ROOM

Scene A: You, in the powder room at Patty Freakin' Perfect's manor house. Your hands are dripping wet. You reach for a hand towel and discover . . . antique linen guest towels pressed to the flatness of parchment, folded into perfect thirds. These towels bear the monogram of the Perfect clan, or perhaps the Perfect coat of arms. You wonder, *Is this here towel for me, the guest, to . . . use?* Can you dry your hands with something like this? Is this a test?

You flap your hands around, wipe them on your hips, and daintily pat the bottom hem of the finger towel as if to say, *I used this finger towel, but I didn't muss it up.*

Scene B: You, in the bathroom used by Betty Playgroup's five growing boys. Your hands are dripping wet. You reach for a hand towel and discover . . . a damp Spongebob Squarepants beach towel drooping over the tub. *Well,* you think warily, *this corner probably doesn't have throw-up on it.*

We humbly suggest that there exists a middle ground here, a hand towel that harkens to the prissed-out finger towels of yore, yet provides the modern-day absorbency of a Spongebob Squarepants beach towel. This hand towel is large enough that you'll have dry hands after using it, and you won't have ruined some towel presser's day. And, because it's made of luxurious, durable linen, it qualifies as an heirloom that even Patty would be proud to hand down to the little Perfects. If you have the urge to make sets of hand towels for all the holidays of the year—an impulse that has existed since Helen of Troy gussied up the bathroom before Paris came over—well, be our guest and go to it.

We happen to like the way these look, too. Linen washes and dries like a dream and lasts forever. (Linen cloth has been found, intact, in the tombs of the ancient Egyptians—we're not sure it was fashioned into hand towels, though.) But feel free to substitute an absorbent cotton yarn if you wish. Gauge is not crucial, but keep in mind that the dimensions of the towel will vary with different weights of yarn.

THINGS THAT
LOOK HARD
BUT AREN'T:
• BUTTONHOLES
• ATTACHING
  A SLEEVE
• PICKING UP
  STITCHES

THIS PAGE: A batch of these linen hand towels would make a tender present for a bride.
RIGHT PAGE: We'd like to do an Outward Bound–style exercise in which we all knit with stiff linen yarn, wash it, see how drapey it turns, and start crying because we all *trusted the yarn*.

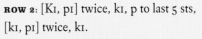

MOSS GRID HAND TOWEL

SIZE: 13" x 20" (33 cm x 51 cm)

MATERIALS: Euroflax Originals sport weight by Louet Sales, [3½ oz (100g) hanks, each approx 270 yds (247 m), linen] 1 hank
Size 5 (3.75 mm) needles or size needed to achieve gauge

GAUGE: 20 sts + 28 rows = 4" (10 cm) over St st.

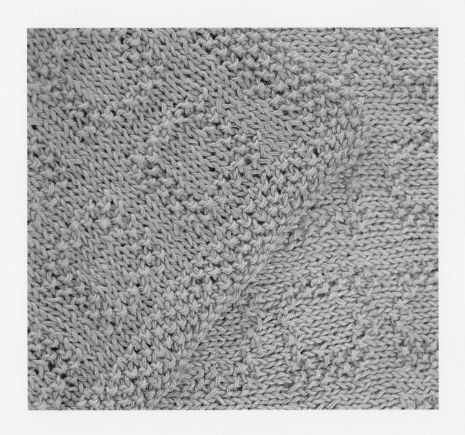

CO 73 sts.

Create Moss Stitch Border, as follows:

ROW 1: K1, *p1, k1; rep from * to end.

ROWS 2-6: Repeat 1.

Begin Moss Grid pattern:

ROW 1: [K1, p1] twice, k to last 4 sts, [p1, k1] twice.

ROW 2: [K1, p1] twice, k1, p to last 5 sts, [k1, p1] twice, k1.

These 2 rows establish a 5-stitch border of moss stitch at the beginning and end of each row. (Suggestion: Place a marker after the first 5 stitches and before the last 5 stitches.) The instructions that follow begin with the 6th stitch of each row and end when there are 5 stitches left.

ROW 3: K4, *[p1, k1] 3 times, p1, k5; rep from * to last 11 sts, [p1, k1] 3 times, p1, k4.

ROW 4: P3, *[k1, p1] 4 times, k1, p3; rep from * to end.

ROW 5: K4, *p1, k5; rep from * to last 5 sts, p1, k4.

ROW 6: P3, *k1, p7, k1, p3; rep from * to end.

ROWS 7, 9, AND 11: Repeat Row 5.

ROWS 8 AND 10: Repeat Row 6.

ROW 12: Repeat Row 4.

ROW 13: Repeat Row 3.

ROW 14: Purl.

Repeat these 14 rows 11 more times.

NEXT ROW: [K1, p1] twice, k to last 4 sts, [p1, k1] twice.

Work 6 rows in moss stitch, then BO in moss stitch.

CHEVRON STRIPES HAND TOWEL

These refined towels prove that the humble stitch dictionary is the great new way to fill your linen closet with elegant stuff. If you tire of squares or chevrons after a couple of hand towels, poke around in your Barbara Walker treasury or one of those Eight-Zillion-Stitch-Patterns-a-Year calendars.

SIZE: 14" x 24" (35 cm x 61 cm)

MATERIALS: Euroflax Originals sport weight by Louet Sales [3½ oz (100g) hanks, each approx 270yds (247 m), linen], 1 hank in light blue (A) and 1 hank in sage green (B)
Size 5 (3.75 mm) needles or size needed to achieve gauge

GAUGE: 20 sts + 28 rows = 4" (10 cm) over St st.
With A, CO 87 sts.

Begin Chevron Stripes pattern:

With A, work 5 rows garter st (knit every row).

ROW 6 (RS): Using B, *k2tog, k2, kfb in next 2 sts, k3, SKP; rep from * to last 5 sts, k5.

ROW 7: K5, purl to last 5 sts, k5.

Repeat rows 6 and 7 two times.

ROW 12: Using A instead of B, rep row 6.

Alternating A and B as set, rep these 12 rows 26 times, then repeat rows 1-5. BO.

The panels of seed stitch on the front yoke can be as colorful or subtle as you like. And the dragon scales on the edge can go very girly if done in the Official Shades of Girls Under Eight: pink, purple, or pinkandpurple.

PLEASE, STEP AWAY FROM THE RHINESTONES

A new knitter tends to have Fear of Finishing. Sewing up seams and attaching sleeves are not the reasons most people start knitting. It is rare to hear "Hey, guess what! I just took up seaming! It is *so* much fun!" When you're just starting out, it's hard enough to keep an even tension, so we have devised a project that allows you the satisfaction of a garment without all that garmenty fussiness: the little decorated jean jacket. The hard part is done—all that is required is for you to get in touch with your inner Bedazzler.

Think of this pint-size purchased jacket as a delivery system for whatever small knitting experiments you want to make. You will be able to embark on techniques that you are not ready to attempt on a larger scale. Intarsia? Fair Isle? Lace? You can do anything for four inches.

Cristina Shiffman took our germ of an idea and made it into portable works of art that make us crazy with delight. While these jackets may appear to be the work of a gifted shut-in who has spent three years on each element, the fact is that these designs can be made by anyone. Even, yes, a beginner who has curiosity and a dash of fortitude. Dive in, and you will see what we mean.

Intarsia? Fair Isle? *Lace?* You can do anything for four inches.

It doesn't take a stretch
of the imagination to
see the possibilities in
decorating a jean jacket
for a full-size human,
namely yourself.
Putting denim yarn
decorations on a denim
jacket is a tone-on-tone
texturefest.

Intarsia really isn't an orthopedic bone problem—it's how you get small dragons to show up on jean jackets. Relatively painless. No crutches required.

DRAGON JACKET

By Cristina Shiffman

Where did this dragon come from? Cristina explains: "The colors of the Kureyon inspired the dragon jacket. I'm very much a dive-right-in knitter. I love that Noro yarns don't have names but only numbers so you're not persuaded by a title to use the yarn a certain way. The blue-green said 'dragon' to me, and I was sitting down with a piece of graph paper within minutes to work out the intarsia on the back."

The Dragon Jacket is designed for size 18–24 months, with a waist measurement of 27 inches when closed. You can use a different size jacket and adjust the knitted embellishments to fit. To adjust the length of the waistband edging, knit more or fewer garter-stitch points, checking for correct length by holding or pinning the edging against the bottom hem of the jacket as you knit. For the back and front patches, you need not make any changes to the intarsia charts; add or subtract background stitches or rows around the edges of the pieces so that they will fit onto your jacket, bearing in mind that each inch (2.5 cm) equals 5 stitches or 7 rows.

MATERIALS: Kureyon by Noro, [1¾ oz (50 g) skeins, each approx 109 yds (100 m), wool] 1 skein in blue/green multi; Lamb's Pride 1-Ply Worsted by Brown Sheep, [4 oz (113 g) skeins, each approx 190yds (173 m), wool/mohair] 1 skein in turquoise; Felted Tweed by Rowan Yarns, [1¾ oz (50 g) balls, each approx 191yds (175 m), merino wool/alpaca/viscose/rayon] 1 ball each in navy and green

Sewing thread, dark blue

Sizes 4 and 7 (3.5 mm and 4.5 mm) needles or size needed to achieve gauge
GAUGE: 20 sts + 28 rows = 4" (10 cm) over St st.

Dragon Scale Edging

Using Kureyon and larger needles, CO 7 sts and work edging as follows:

ROW 1: K4, yo, k3.

ROW 2 AND ALL WS ROWS: Knit.

ROW 3: K4, yo, k4.

ROW 5: K4, yo, k5.

ROW 7: K4, yo, k6.

ROW 9: K4, yo, k7.

ROW 11: K4, yo, k8.

ROW 12: BO 6 sts, k6 (7 sts).

Repeat Rows 1-12 11 more times, or until edging is long enough to fit around bottom edge of jacket. BO.

Finishing

To give a fuzzy, dense texture, lightly felt the edging by handwashing it in hot water with dishwashing liquid, rubbing it, and rinsing in cold water. To avoid shrinkage, *do not felt in a washing machine.*

Sew into place on the inside bottom edge of jacket, positioning the ends of the edging so that the dragon scales meet but do not overlap when the jacket is snapped shut.

Dragon Panel for Jacket Back

Using Kureyon and size 4 (3.5 mm) needles, CO 52 sts. Work intarsia chart Rows 1-30 in St st, using Kureyon for the background and Lamb's Pride for the dragon.

Handwash as described for edging, press, and embroider the dragon's back spines, wings, and tail tip using oddments of Felted Tweed and embroidery stitches.

Using dark blue sewing thread, whipstitch and backstitch this panel onto the jacket back, slightly easing and stretching the panel as needed to fit the shoulder contours.

Dragon Skin Patches for Front of Jacket
(Make 2)

With Kureyon and smaller needles, CO 23 sts.

Work 2 rows in seed stitch: *K1, p1; repeat from * to end of row.

Next row and all following rows: Repeat Row 1.

AT THE SAME TIME, work 2 tog at beginning of third row and every fourth row thereafter until 15 sts remain.

BO in seed stitch.

Finishing

Handwash as described for edging, press, and whipstitch into place.

Crown and Castle Sleeve Patches

Using Felted Tweed and smaller needles, CO 26 stitches in background color. Complete the chart and BO.

Finishing

Handwash as described for edging, press, and whipstitch onto sleeves.

Optional Lining

For extra warmth, felt an old wool sweater to line the inside back of the jacket. Cut a sweater piece the right width and approximate length, and attach to the bottom edge using blanket stitch. Then cut the top edge to fit more precisely, and whipstitch the remaining 3 edges of the lining into place.

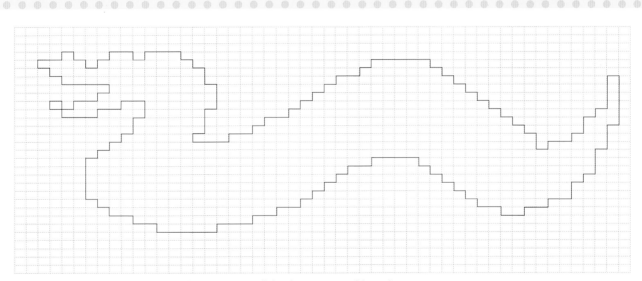

For the dragon, work the background in Kureyon and the dragon in Lamb's Pride.

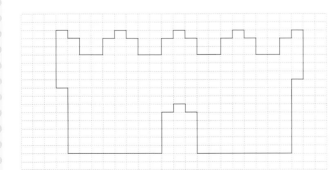

For the castle, work the background in green and the castle in navy.

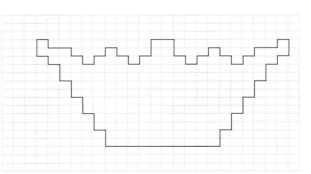

For the crown, work the background in navy and the crown in green.

FLOWER JACKET

By Cristina Shiffman

Don't worry! The instructions look long here, but none of them are hard. You will get great experience at following a pattern.

The flower jacket is embellished with one pansy (front), one daisy patch (sleeve), and a posy of three cosmos (back). You can combine these elements as shown or any other way that you like. You can also add lace edgings or ruffles to the bottom, cuffs, or collar if you wish (see instructions for the Dragon Jacket and Moses Basket: Stovetop Version for edging ideas, or consult a stitch dictionary for more ideas—there are many choices). Here are the instructions for the elements shown on the jacket in the photograph.

Use bits of yarns that you have on hand to make these little flowers. For the cosmos in our example, we used a single skein of Noro Kureyon, a self-striping, multicolored yarn. The different colors were separated into strands of related colors. This way we got three flowers of different colors from a single skein of yarn. Clever, no?

MATERIALS: Any worsted weight yarn in shades of your choosing. We used oddments of Cascade 220 Wool by Cascade Yarns, [3½ oz (100 g) hanks, each approx 220 yds (201 m), wool] and Kureyon by Noro, [1¾ oz (50 g) hanks, each approx 109 yds (100 m), wool]
Size 3 or 4 (3.25 mm or 3.5 mm) needles
Double-pointed needles
Crochet hook

GAUGE: Doesn't matter.

The flowers are so dimensional. Depending on the yarn you use, the flowers can pretty much jump off the jacket.

Pansy

Our example uses 3 colors of yarn, A, B, and C.

Small Petal (make 3)

Using A, CO 2 sts.

ROW 1: Using B, kfb, k1 (3 sts).

ROW 2: Purl.

ROW 3: Kfb, kfb, k1 (5 sts).

ROW 4: Purl.

ROW 5: Using C, kfb, change to B, k2, change to C, kfb, change to B, k1 (7 sts).

ROW 6: Using C, p3, change to B, p1, change to C, p3.

ROW 7: Using C, [k1, kfb] 3 times, k1 (10 sts).

ROW 8: Purl.

ROW 9: Ssk, knit to last 2 sts, k2tog (8 sts).

ROW 10: BO in purl.

Large Petal (make 2)

Using B, CO 2 sts.

ROW 1: Kfb, k1 (3 sts).

ROW 2 AND ALL WS ROWS: Purl.

ROW 3: Kfb, kfb, k1 (5 sts).

ROW 5: Kfb, k3, kfb (7 sts).

ROW 7: [K1, kfb] 3 times, k1 (10 sts).

ROW 9: Knit.

ROW 11: Ssk, knit to last 2 sts, k2tog (8 sts).

ROW 13: Repeat Row 11 (6 sts).

ROW 14: BO in purl.

To Assemble the Pansy

Run yarn through base of each large petal and pull to pucker slightly. Sew petals together side by side, stopping short of outer edge. Sew edges of smaller petals together along their sides. Position small petals over large ones so that the bigger gap of the trio lines up with the gap of the pair. Use a tiny bit of contrasting yarn (we used orange) to embroider a French knot in the center of the flower. Sew in all ends. Sew pansy in place above left front pocket.

Pansy Leaf (make 2)

We used bits of green Cascade 220.

CO 9 sts.

ROWS 1, 3, 5: K3, sl 2tog knitwise, k1, p2sso, k3 (7 sts).

ROWS 2, 4: K1, yf, M1 purlwise, p5, M1 purlwise, k1 (9 sts).

ROW 6: K1, p5, k1.

ROW 7: K2, sl2tog knitwise, k1, p2sso, k2 (5 sts).

ROW 8: K1, p3, k1.

ROW 9: K1, sl 2tog knitwise, k1, p2sso, k1 (3 sts).

ROW 10: K1, p1, k1.

ROW 11: Sl 2tog knitwise, k1, p2sso (1 st).

Fasten off.

Cosmos (make 3)

These look really cool using different shades of yarn cut from the same ball of striping Noro Kureyon, but they would also be cute in mixed or solid colors from your leftovers.

Petals (8 petals per Cosmos)

CO 3 sts.

ROW 1: Kfb, k1, kfb (5 sts).

Work 11 rows in St st, starting and ending with a purl row.

ROW 13: K3, BO 1 st, k1 (4 sts) (the 1-stitch bind-off forms the ridged shape of the end of the petal).

ROW 14: P2tog, holding yarn loosely, p2tog (2 sts).

Fasten off the last 2 sts separately by using a yarn needle and running the yarn into the center of the petal between the 2 sts you are binding off. Tack down the strand of yarn between the last 2 sts to define the cleft at the end of the petal.

Sew 4 petals together in a cross shape, joining them in the center. Repeat with the remaining 4 petals. Position these 2 crosses, one on top of the other, at a 45-degree angle to form the flower. Use a contrasting bit of yarn to make 7 or more French knots at the center of the flower.

Stems and Fronds

Use a crochet hook and green yarn to make long and short chains to form the

stems and fronds of the cosmos as shown in the photograph.

Posy Ribbon

Using dpns or a circular needle, CO 5 sts in a contrasting color. Knit one 15" (38 cm) length of I-cord.

....

What is I-cord?

It's a neat little tube of stitches. Making I-cord is the same thing as knitting in the round on a very small number of stitches. How to make I-cord: CO 5 sts on a dpn or circular needle. Knit the row, then slide all 5 sts to the other end of the needle and knit another row, tugging the working yarn around to the other end of the row. Repeat this until the cord is the correct length, and BO all sts.

To Assemble the Posy of Cosmos

Arrange the flowers, stems, and fronds on the back of the jacket as shown in the illustration (or as pleases your eye) and sew them on with sewing thread. Form the I-cord into a bow shape, and secure the center by winding matching yarn and tying it in the back. Sew the ribbon on top of the stems.

Daisy Arm Patch

Using a light background color (we used lighter colors from the Kureyon), CO 8 sts.

ROW 1: Knit.

ROW 2: Purl.

ROW 3: Kfb, k to last st, kfb (10 sts).

ROW 4: Purl.

Repeat Rows 3 and 4 until there are 16 sts.

Work 9 rows St st, ending with a purl row.

ROW 19: Ssk, knit to last 2 sts, k2tog (14 sts).

ROW 20: Purl.

The daisy embroidery brings a delicate element to this knitted patch.

Repeat Rows 19 and 20 until there are 8 sts, ending with a purl row. BO.

Using a contrasting color of yarn, embroider small daisies. Use a contrasting color to form center of daisies by crossing over the "petal" stitches to secure. Sew patch into place on sleeve.

AN ENDLESS CURIOSITY: Cristina Shiffman

On any given day, Cristina Shiffman is likely to be found making linoleum block prints at her kitchen table, folding origami, or scheming up dragons to knit. There's handmade stuff all over her Philadelphia house. We love that.

Q: Where do you get this creative impulse?

A: It's probably the semantics snob in me coming out, but "creative" is a word that troubles me because it implies producing something from nothing. Everything I do begins with my fascination with some material like those three balls of mohair yarn or some sheets of lovely paper. Unless I'm happily following a pattern, I just have to let myself start doing something with the stuff and not form a plan that can be analyzed and critiqued to ruins. I think I'm in the mad-scientist end of the makers' spectrum. I'm not particularly organized or meticulous. But I'm crazy about good yarn, clay, beads, paper, felt—you name it—so a failure doesn't get me down for long because there's always more stuff to work with.

Q: What's your favorite sort of knitting?

A: I like texture. I've particularly enjoyed the Aran sweaters I've knitted because I think it's amazing that our fingers actually know what to do after getting once or twice through a twenty-row pattern repeat. Fair Isle knitting in the round is sort of the same for me. Alice Starmore is my idea of a knitting genius. Kim Hargreaves is also a big favorite. And I find myself going to Elizabeth Zimmermann more and more often as I make up my own designs and make changes to patterns.

Q: A pretty traditional group, don't you think?

A: They are working within "the tradition," if you want to give it that hifalutin' name, but still making beautiful and interesting things to knit. It seems to me that the designers I like most understand that. Kim Hargreaves I like for the way she uses textured stitch patterns and shaping. Alice Starmore can use color like no one else can. And Elizabeth Zimmermann I like to read to gain encouragement to make up my own patterns. She took joy from her craft, and it shows in her writing and in her designs.

Q: What would you say to a new knitter?

A: I would give the advice I got from the woman who started me off: scarves are great, but starting with a pattern for a sweater that you'd love to wear is absolutely within the realm of the possible for the beginner, and the learning curve is gratifyingly steep. The first thing I cast on was a big, shirtlike cardigan by Kim Hargreaves. I couldn't afford the Rowan yarn, so I substituted, and it turned out like something that would look good on a lumberjack if he happened to like bright teal blue. I ripped the whole thing up, which was one of the more character building things ever to happen to me. I reknitted the yarn as a very plain drop-shoulder turtleneck that I made up as I went along.

The first time I wore it, a friend admired it so much I gave it to her on the spot. It was then I realized I was as much process as project oriented. It might be the satisfaction with making that I would want the new knitter to discover with happy surprise.

Q: Yes—that happy surprise is what gets people hooked, and it doesn't matter whether they're creating something complex or simple. Some of the most inspiring knitters I know would not fall into the category of Expert Knitters—they'd rather die than fuss with a Fair Isle sweater.

A: You make a good point about being "good" not being

the point about knitting. I always try to explain to people who think knitting must be difficult that pretty much all knitting is just learning how to knit and purl; and purling is just knitting the opposite way. At first you get over how awkward it feels to hold the needles and yarn; then your brain gets used to the spatial dynamics; then maybe you have to loosen up or tighten up. The next thing you know, for crying out loud, you've MADE fabric.

Q: I find I'm still interested in the technical aspects of it all—who in the world figured out all these things?

A: It seems that Mother Necessity answers for most. What I want to know is: How did the idea that continuously looping yarn through itself would make fabric occur to the Mother of All Knitters? For that matter, how did it occur to someone to cut a sheep's coat, comb the fleece, and spin the strands? Have you ever tried spinning? There's not a whole lot about a pile of right-off-the-sheep fleece that suggests it could become yarn.

Q: What is your earliest memory of knitting?

A: Do you know that Sylvester and Tweety cartoon in which Sylvester's black fur comes unraveled and he re-knits it in a bright argyle? That did it for me, though it turned out that intarsia is not as easy as Sylvester makes it look.

With each monthly shipment of squares for our charity project, Cristina sent a handmade card.

MISTAKES YOU WILL DEFINITELY MAKE

★ ★ ★ ★ ★ ★ ★ ★ ★ ★

YOU WILL...
You will drop stitches.

YOU WILL...
knit in the wrong direction.

YOU WILL...
have a crummy-looking edge.

YOU WILL...
have tension issues.

YOU WILL...
increase the number of stitches in a row without intending to.

YOU WILL...
knit too tightly.

YOU WILL...
knit too loosely.

YOU WILL...
have trouble holding the yarn right.

YOU WILL...
tangle a skein of yarn into an octopuslike mess.

YOU WILL...
forget to decrease.

YOU WILL...
forget to increase.

Kay

HOW TO COPE WITH DISASTER: SAVE THE EVIDENCE

Every knitter—and we do mean every knitter—leaves in her wake an unspeakable mess. Oh sure, whenever you bump into Patty Freakin' Perfect at the Dee-Lux Palais de Yarn, she's wearing a Kaffe Fassett overcoat that she has embellished with Alice Starmore trimmings and gussied up with a few of Barbara Walker's toughest edgings. But back at Casa de Patty, under her bed or lurking in her pristine closets, is a nasty cardboard box crammed with dangly swatches, hole-ridden false starts, and hunchbacked sweaters that will never see the light of day.

Why does Patty keep these reminders of past trauma? Because a knitter cannot bring herself to get rid of anything that she has made with her own two hands. This is one of the unspoken laws of the coven: Every handknit is precious.

So the question arises: What do you do with all this crap? You save it. Or even better, you figure out a way to use it. If it's wool, throw it in the washing machine, set it to hot wash/cold rinse, and let 'er rip. Chances are, this will felt the piece, which you can then cut up (yes, you can cut wool that's been felted into a state of dense chewiness) into squares or other shapes, and then sew together into patchwork rugs or blankets. Voilà: instant, cushy folk art. If the piece is not feltable, you can rip it out and reuse the yarn. Whatever you do, don't throw anything away. You might *need* it someday.

You see: a godawful
mess of swatches.
We see: the exciting
proof of creative
expression and—euw,
what is that creepy
Fair Isle thing in there?

Chapter Two

KNITTING * AROUND THE HOUSE

My house isn't picky: IT DOESN'T CARE IF THAT AFGHAN IS **A LITTLE TOO BIG,** or the wrong color. IT IS THE MOST FORGIVING recipient of stuff **I * KNIT,** AND IT WILL WEAR IT UNTIL *I* GET TIRED of looking at it.

Ann ✳ We come now to the red-hot core, the deep-down, soul-shakin' epicenter of knitting in the Mason-Dixon style. I peer into my closet. I see all sorts of things: A fishing rod. The shoes I wore at my wedding. A stainless steel bowl full of candy that I hid in 2001 a week after Halloween so that the boys would stop eating chocolate eyeballs. Ah, what's this? An heirloom more treasured even than the shoes I wore at my wedding: a ski sweater my mother knitted in 1958. And looky—another sweater she knitted who knows when. What else? Seven tender and meaningful sweaters I knitted for myself, moldering away in the gloom.

It's a regular Ripley's Believe It or Not in there, a curiosity shoppe of the sacred and profane all piled together willy-nilly. Nobody goes in there much except for me. Nobody sees the sweater with the dreadlocky nubbin fringe I made—my portable tribute to Bob Marley—or the six-foot-long shawl that represents six weeks of sitting in the blazing sun watching Clif figure out how to swim. Nobody sees most of the things I've spent hour upon hour cranking out—it's hard to wear your handknits enough, to admire your handiwork enough, to get your kids to wear the stuff you have made.

This is why I have turned more and more to knitting stuff for my house to wear. My house isn't picky: My house doesn't complain if a Shetland wool cushion is kind of scratchy. It doesn't care if that afghan is a little too big, or too small, or the wrong color. It is the most forgiving recipient of stuff I knit, and it will wear it until I get tired of looking at it.

KNITTING THAT LOOKS LIKE SOMETHING ELSE

If you look around my house, you find stuff made by women in my family who are no longer here. They've gone to a better place, but their compulsively needlepointed chair cushions live on.

Right now I'm thinking about my mother, Helen; my grandmother Gilmore, known as Grommy; and Hubbo's grandmother Mary Jane. Despite their wildly differing lives, each lived in the 1960s, so they shared one trait with all women who lived in the 1960s: the urge to cover chairs with needlepoint upholstery.

At one point, my mother and her mother needlepointed ten dining-room chair seats, in an epic project that lasted through the Johnson administration, the early Nixon years, and the landing of a man on the moon. This project instilled in me the notion that no project is too ambitious if you crave the result enough. Mom wanted needlepointed dining-room chairs. She got them.

I got to thinking about knitting that doesn't look like knitting. Because I don't enjoy making needlepoint, I started to mess around with knitting patterns that looked like

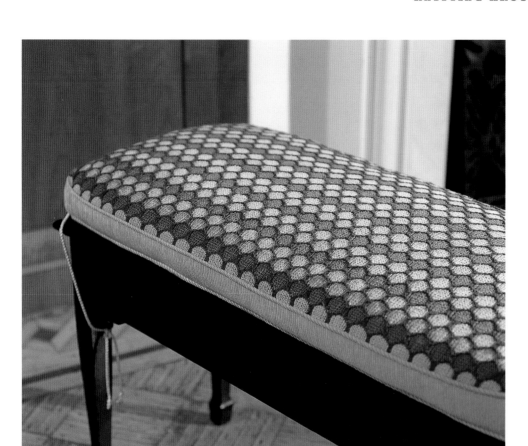

In the matter of cushion-making, consider how your cushion will be used. The box edge here looks all formal and tidy, but a knife-edge cushion might stand up better to the Grand Canyon-like effect of fidgety pianists sitting on it.

INSPIRATION
The multitude of shades in old rugs is a constant amazement. Once the vegetable dyes have faded, you see the stop-and-start of the rugmaker where a new skein was added. It was a thrill to find yarn for the cushion that was at home with the mellow colors of this carpet.

needlepoint, or crewelwork, or anything that didn't instantly read "knitted" when you looked at it. I wanted to have knitting in the living room, but my living room is not an obvious haven for handknits. Nothing in there seemed to require a handknit, or would even benefit from one. Hard to imagine, but true.

When Hubbo's beloved grandfather Albert died, and Big Daddy's piano ended up in our living room, opportunity arrived. The bench, a plain black bench, cried out for a cushion. With the instincts of a beaver studying a free-flowing stream, I knew what I had to do.

I like the idea of a knitted cushion on a chair that's asking for brocade. There are stitch patterns that look for all the world like crewelwork, or needlepoint, or even bargello. Slip stitches can create all sorts of smocky-looking patterns, stuff that looks great on a cushion. And once you start picking up a stitch from three rows below, well, it gets crazy.

The trick is to find stitch patterns that create fabric with some bulk—a single thickness of stockinette is probably not going to hold up, unless it's a chunky yarn or if it's done as a flat cushion.

Danny the Magnificent Upholsterer is famed in Nashville for re-covering Tammy Wynette's sectional sofa in 1974. (OK, not really.) He edged the piece of knitting with interfacing to provide a steady, nonstretchy edge for his sewing machine. The one-inch margin was just enough for him to work his magic.

BIG DOTTY CUSHION

A cushion for sitting needs to be made of sturdy stuff, which is what led me to linen yarn. I figure if linen is good enough for the Shroud of Turin, it'll do for this piano bench cushion.

FINISHED SIZE: 15" x 36" (38 cm x 91.5 cm); cushion top before finishing: 17" x 38" (43 cm x 96.5 cm)

MATERIALS: Euroflax Originals sport weight by Louet Sales, [3½ oz (100 g) hanks, each approx 270 yds (247 m), linen] 2 hanks each in rust (A), champagne (B), dark gray (C), and light gray (D)

Size 3 (3.25 mm) circular needle or size needed to achieve gauge. (You can use straights if you're making a small cushion. But why not use a circular? You'll never lose a needle!)

GAUGE: 24 sts = 4" (10 cm) over pat st. Make a swatch 8" (20.5 cm) square so that you can get a good measurement. This slip-stitch pattern pulls vertically quite a bit, so your results may vary.

CO 228 sts.

Knit two rows in D, then begin the Big Dotty stitch pattern as follows:

ROWS 1 AND 2: Row 1 is RS. Using A, knit.

ROW 3: Using B, k1, slip 2 (slip all sts purlwise), *k6, slip 2; rep from * to the last st, k1.

ROW 4: Using B, p1, slip 2, *p6, slip 2; rep from * to last st, p1.

ROWS 5-8: Repeat Rows 3 and 4 twice more.

ROWS 9 AND 10: Using A, knit.

ROW 11: Using C, k5, slip 2, *k6, slip 2; rep from * to last 5 sts, k5.

ROW 12: Using C, p5, slip 2, *p6, slip 2; rep from * to last 5 sts, p5.

ROWS 13-16: Repeat Rows 11 and 12 twice more.

Repeat Rows 1-16 for pattern, replacing B with D and replacing C with B.

Keep at it, alternating the background colors in this pattern. When piece is 17", end the pattern with Rows 1 and 2, knitting two final rows in whatever color

Eeek! Before it's blocked, Big Dotty is Big Puckered Mess.

comes next in the background color pattern. BO.

This piece requires stout blocking to flatten the patternwork. Wet it thoroughly and pin it carefully. After it's been pinned for a month or two (OK, a day or two if you're in a hurry), send it off to the upholsterer with 2 yds (2m) of a coordinating, sturdy upholstery fabric. Or make the cushion yourself if you know how. The cushion is filled with 2" (5 cm) foam wrapped with batting. The welting keeps it looking tidy. The upholsterer added ties at each of the corners to hold the cushion in place on the bench.

WHO DOESN'T NEED A
LITTLE PADDING?

★ ★ ★ ★ ★ ★ ★ ★ ★ ★ ★ ★ ★

Any hard chair can benefit from a cushion like this. Think of a Windsor chair with a flat, matlike piece. A ladderback chair with a thin cushion tied to the back. A caned chair with a thick, stout cushion, with button tufting for that fancy look. A child's chair with a tiny, colorful square. Find a chair! Cushion it!

TECHNICAL HINT

The Cushion You Want ★ **To make a Big Dotty cushion to fit your chair, measure the chair you plan to top with this cushion. Add 1" (2.5 cm) for seaming to all four sides. Now you have your dimensions. To calculate how many stitches to cast on, remember that every inch requires 6 stitches. And make sure you cast on a multiple of 8 stitches plus 4 so that the pattern works right.**

Holding your knitting up to the sun—
we do it all the time. A curtain lets you
admire the light through your lace forever.

Neighbors would see a *symphony of white* and think,

TWILIGHT IN NASHVILLE

One warm, dark evening last summer, I stood in our bathtub. Taped to the windows above the tub were six pieces of cloth: sheer, kind of sheer, sort of sheer, not so sheer, unsheer, and slightly-less-sheer-than-plywood sheer. My assignment was to stand behind each piece of fabric and pretend to be naked and getting out of the tub.

"Nope. I can see you very clearly." Hubbo was out in the yard. He was speaking softly into his cell phone. I had my phone wedged between ear and shoulder.

"This?" I was waving around like an extra in an Esther Williams movie.

"No good."

"How about this?" Panel number three. I held up two fingers.

"Two."

Damn. We moved down the samples, inexorably, to the only panel that would obviously solve this problem, the panel that obliterated the beautiful green view high above my bathtub.

"Bingo," he says. "That's what I'm talkin' 'bout."

Once again, the triumph of function over form. Hubbo was delighted. The negotiation began.

When we moved to this house a few years ago, Hubbo began a never-ending study of our house's privacy problems. Hubbo does not want to be seen by anyone who might be passing by our house. As with so many issues in our marriage, the more concerned he is, the more I adopt the opposite attitude. "Windows, shmindows," I'd say. "I don't care if the Lefkowitzes see me nekkid in the bathroom—who cares? I love the Lefkowitzes! And we're all nekkid under our clothes anyway, right?"

Our house has a fair number of windows, so I spend a fair amount of time trying to cover them up. I have wooden blinds, metal blinds, roller shades, Roman shades, shutters, draperies, and in some cases, nothing at all. I think about window treatments the way Ben and Jerry think about ice cream. Anything's possible, right? Wouldn't an airy, knitted curtain be lovely in my bathroom? Wouldn't that just solve it all? Neighbors zooming by at thirty miles an hour would see a symphony of white and think, *What a relief not to see Ann Shayne getting out of that tub anymore.*

Well, a year later, I have made some discoveries, the chief one being that it is actually possible to knit a curtain.

CURTAIN RULES

THE CURTAIN MUST be small.

THE CURTAIN MUST be made of a non-boingy yarn.

THE CURTAIN MUST be a fine gauge.

THE CURTAIN MUST be starched, and starched mightily.

The curtain will never achieve Holiday Inn rubbery blackout curtain perfection. It is an adornment, a decoration, a place where you can try a lace pattern and admire it for a very long time. Take a look around: See? There's a kitchen window, a small bathroom window, that weird little window on your front door—you can pretend you're a French country lady.

"What a relief not to see Ann Shayne getting out of that tub anymore."

Mason-Dixon Rule Number 72:

NO PROJECT IS TOO AMBITIOUS IF YOU CRAVE THE RESULT ENOUGH

BUBBLY CURTAIN

The idea for this pattern came from staring idly, as one does, at a flute of champagne. The bubbles tend to originate in one spot at the bottom and travel upward in columns. If you have one of those tall, narrow side windows by your door, this could get really intoxicating.

Bubbly is the sort of curtain that can be used for any small window. If you're shooting to cover a giant bay window, a trip to the Target window treatment aisle may be a better choice. The simple yarnover/k2tog charted pattern can be repeated as many times as necessary across the width of the curtain, and the top four rows can be repeated to fill out the curtain.

SIZE: 20" x 18" (51 cm x 45 cm)

MATERIALS: Euroflax Originals sport weight by Louet Sales, [3½ oz (100 g) hanks, each approx 270 yds (247 m), linen], 2 hanks beige
Size 5 (3.75 mm) needles or size needed to achieve gauge

GAUGE: 20 sts + 26 rows = 4" (10 cm) over St st.

Note: The curtain has a 5-stitch garter stitch edge at both sides.

CO 100 stitches.

Knit 4 rows.

NEXT ROW: K5. Follow Row 1 (RS) of chart. Chart is knitted in St st. Repeat the 18-stitch pattern 5 times, then k5.

NEXT ROW: Purl. Continue as set, knitting the first and last 5 stitches of every row, following the chart for all RS rows and purling all WS rows. After completing all rows of the chart, repeat rows 71-118 to fill height of curtain.

When curtain is 1" (2.5 cm) short of its final height, make a row of eyelets for threading the twisted cord: K5, *yo, k2tog, k4 until last 5 sts of row, k5.

Knit final four rows to complete garter stitch border of curtain.

Finishing

This is one of the times when a sure-nuff pin-blocking fiesta pays off. Soak your curtain well, get the pins out, and teach that curtain who's boss. The bubbles open up, the warbly stitches start to behave, and your curtain will improve like crazy. Once the pins are in, you must decide the burning question:

starch or no starch? It's like men's shirts. People have strong feelings about these things. I love the way spray starch provides structure to the knitting and helps it behave. But then, I love spray starch in general.

The cord at the top is a simple twisted cord made from the same yarn as the curtain. Find a doorknob, a hook, or a willing finger. Affix the yarn to it, at least four times the length of the finished cord you desire, and start twisting the cord. Eventually it will double back on itself to make a beautiful, tight cord. We love this trick. Our friend Robin Smith has used an electric mixer for fast results, but we aren't that brave. Tie the ends together, snip the extra, and thread the cord through the eyelets. Tie each end to the loop next to it. Find a twig, a dowel, or forge yourself an iron rod. Hang. Open bottle of effervescent beverage.

TECHNICAL HINT

Your Own Custom Bubbly Curtain ★ Measure the window for which you're making the curtain. Decide whether you want the curtain to fit inside the window frame or if you want it to extend to the edge of the trimwork. The vertical measurement should allow room for the curtain rod and the cord that attaches the curtain to the rod. Make the width of your curtain a multiple of 18 stitches plus 10 for the 5-stitch garter stitch border on each side. And make a gauge swatch to be sure you're getting 5 stitches to the inch.

REHABILITATING THE
TARTY
11½" FASHION DOLL

Bubbly Curtain Chart

18-Stitch Repeat. Repeat pattern above bold
line as often as necessary to fill.

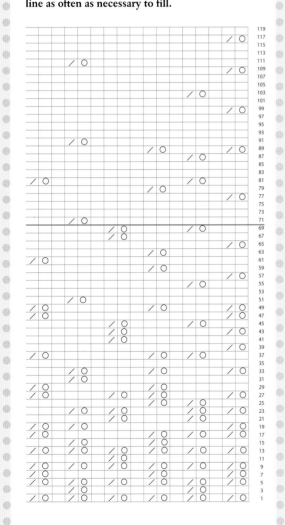

Stitch Key:
▢ = Knit
◪ = K2tog
◎ = Yo

Ann ✳ When I was growing up, I loved 11½"
fashion dolls. There was no Wizard of Oz fashion
doll, no Audrey Hepburn fashion doll; there was just
the 11½", in a swimsuit, with high-heel pink shoes.
You bought outfits for your one, or two, or three dolls
if you were kind of spoiled.

One recent Presidents' Day, I had an emergency
playgroup that involved seven minivans, eighteen
children, a group of desperate mothers, and three
pots of coffee. Included in this group were a bunch
of little girls, and when it became apparent that
a house with two boys meant no toys for girls,
I brought out my ancient fashion dolls.

Off the girls went to the playroom, where they
put together many different outfits for the dolls:
the Hooker Doll, with see-through negligee and
thigh-high silver lamé boots; Pan Am Stewardess
Doll; and Gigolo Boyfriend, with a blue satin
tuxedo jacket worthy of any 1972 prom.

As I cleaned up, I found at the bottom of the

pile of clothes a tiny
raglan-sleeve sweater
my mother had knitted,
in sensible charcoal
and cream.
It makes me laugh to
think of my mom seeing
my boxful of tarty doll
clothes and thinking,
"What that doll needs is
a cardigan."

We love the robe and nightie together. We see this and think peignoir. When's the last time you knitted a peignoir?

MASON-DIXON AFTER DARK

Ladies, let's head into the Red Tent for a little all-female conversation. (Fellas, go herd some sheep or something—we'll be done soon. And no, we didn't prepare a meal for you, so go rustle up some of your own lamb flavored with coriander marinated in sour goat milk with a pomegranate sauce for dipping.)

No, Zilpah, we are not going over the midwifery guidelines again. Leah, enough with the unguents—we are all moisturized, OK? Our cup runneth over, OK?

We are here today to talk about raiment. Evening raiment. It has come to my attention that we as a tribe of Old Testament women are in jeopardy of *letting ourselves go.* Look at us! Jacob is going to start looking for a fifth wife if we don't get our act together. If I see one more flannel nightgown out there when the menfolk are around, I mean it—I will personally rend those garments, soak them in cumin oil, and offer them up to the goddess Taweret in hopes of obtaining foxier nightclothes.

Women of the tribe, listen to me. I was reading in *How to Make Love Like an Egyptian* that husbands see their wives mostly at night, and that raiment worn at night should be rilly special. You know, raiment *without* football team logos.

So. This is the plan. We're going to collect all the flax we can, spin it into yarn, dye it a tarty eggplant color, and we're going to cook up some nightgowns and robes that will ice our status as superfoxes of the Holy Land.

"Excuse me while I slip into something a little more . . . handknitted."

MASON-DIXON AFTER-DARK NIGHTIE

By Alison Green Will

We bring you this R-rated item as proof that even a couple of hard-knittin' soccer moms can get it on. This summery nightie makes the most of this beautiful linen yarn, and we like that you can choose the length to match your late-night movie viewing: *The Sound of Music* or *Eyes Wide Shut.*

Knitted Measurements

Bust: 32 (34½, 37, 39, 42, 44)" (81 [87.5, 94, 99, 106.5, 111.5] cm)

Hip: 34 (37, 40, 42, 44, 48)" (86.5 [94, 101.5, 106.5, 111.5, 122] cm)

Length (not including straps): 23½ (23½, 24½, 26, 26, 26)" (59.5 [59.5, 62, 66, 66, 66] cm)

SIZE: To fit XS (S, M, L, XL, XXL). Directions are for smallest size with larger sizes in parentheses. If there is only one figure, it applies to all sizes.

MATERIALS: Euroflax Originals sport weight by Louet Sales, [3½ oz (100 g) hanks, each approx 270 yds (247 m), linen] 3 (3, 3, 4, 4, 5) hanks in violet Sizes 4 and 5 (3.5 mm and 3.75 mm) needles or size needed to achieve gauge Bra Straps. Available from supply stores, or cut them off an existing bra. Matching thread; needle

GAUGE: 20 sts + 32 rows = 4" (10 cm) over St st using size 5 (3.75 mm) needles.

Special Abbreviations

SK2P = slip 1, k2tog, pass slipped st over (a double-decrease).

W&T = wrap and turn: bring the yarn to the front, slip the next st, bring the yarn to the back, slip the st back to the left-hand needle, turn the work.

Back

With size 4 (3.5 mm) needles, CO 85 (94, 103, 112, 112, 121) sts.

Work 3 rows garter st. Change to size 5 (3.37 mm) needles and begin Vine Lace pattern:

ROW 1 (RS): K3, *yo, k2, ssk, k2tog, k2, yo, k1; rep from *, end k1.

ROW 2: Purl.

ROW 3: K2, *yo, k2, ssk, k2tog, k2, yo, k1; rep from *, end k2.

ROW 4: Purl.

Repeat Rows 1-4 until piece measures 5" (12.5 cm). Change to St st and dec 1 (0, 3, 6, 0, 1) st evenly over next row—84 (94, 100, 106, 112, 120) sts. Work even in St st until piece measures 14 (14, 15, 15, 16, 16)" (35.5 (35.5, 38, 38, 40.5, 40.5) cm). Begin waist shaping: Dec 1 st at each end next row, then every 4 rows 5 (5, 5, 6, 6, 6) times more—72 (82, 88, 92, 98, 106) sts. Work even for 1" (2.5 cm). Inc 1 st at each end of next row, then every 6 (12, 12, 8, 8, 12) rows 3 (1, 1, 2, 2, 1) times more—80 (86, 92, 98, 104, 110) sts. Work 4 rows even. Begin Top Border pattern:

For those evenings when a nightgown really is a nightgown, opt for the seed-stitch version. Modest? Yes. But never say never, darlings.

ROW 1 (RS): K1, *k3, yo, SK2P, yo; rep from *, end k1.

ROW 2: Purl.

ROW 3: K1, *yo, SK2P, yo, k3; rep from *, end k1.

ROW 4: Purl.

Repeat Rows 1-4 3 times more. Work 4 rows garter st. BO.

Front

Work as for Back until 3 rows before Top Border pattern. Work short-row bust dart—Next row (RS): Knit to 4 sts before end of row, W&T; purl to 4 sts before end of row, W&T; * knit to 4 sts before wrapped st, W&T; purl to 4 sts before wrapped st, W&T; * rep from * to * 2 more times, knit to end of row, knitting wraps along with wrapped sts. Purl one row, purling rem wraps along with wrapped sts. Knit one row. Work Top Border as for Back.

Finishing

Sew side seams, leaving bottom lace border open on one or both sides. Pin on bra straps to find best placement, then handstitch in place.

The use of adjustable bra straps means that they will not stretch, and the nightgown really will fit.

REQUIEM FOR THE HOUSECOAT

★ ★ ★ ★ ★ ★ ★ ★ ★ ★ ★

KAY · At some point in the Design Process, the realization dawned that what we were making was a refined, fancy-yarn . . . housecoat. Remember housecoats? Mom had one with a quilted satin yoke and a zipper up the front—and that was her young and sassy 1960s housecoat. It smelled like pancakes and was accessorized with a crown of brush rollers. Grandma Mabel's housecoat model was circa 1937 and was still going strong in '72. In a small floral print and a Dust Bowl palette, it had opaque white buttons and short sleeves (the better to use the wringer wash-ing machine). Grandma would never be seen in her house coat after 7 a.m., and while Grandma would sometimes make a sunrise dash out to the clothesline in her house-coat, it otherwise never left the house.

The sash makes an excellent piece of portable knitting. We love the dressmaker detail of the hidden ties inside which close the front in a tidy way.

MASON-DIXON AFTER-DARK ROBE

By Alison Green Will

This robe is sleek enough to wear to that long-anticipated Third Grade Parents' gathering on a hot, sultry night, when the cicadas are whirring and the menfolk are—whoopsy, never mind. Wearing a bathrobe out is so convenient when you get home late and find yourself deciding to sleep in your clothes.

Knitted Measurements

Bust: 40 (46, 52)" (101.5 [117, 132] cm)

Length: 30 (31, 32)" (76 [78.5, 81] cm)

SIZE: To fit Small/Medium (Large, Extra-Large). Directions are for smallest size with larger sizes in parentheses. If there is only one figure, it applies to all sizes.

MATERIALS: Euroflax Originals sport weight by Louet Sales, [3½ oz (100 g)

hanks, each approx 270 yds (247 m), linen] 7 (8, 9) hanks in eggplant
Sizes 4 and 5 (3.5 mm and 3.75 mm) needles or size needed to achieve gauge
Stitch marker
Seam binding or ribbon
GAUGE: 20 sts + 32 rows = 4" (10 cm) over St st using size 5 (3.75 mm) needles.

Back

With size 4 (3.5 mm) needles, CO 100 (116, 130) sts. Work in seed st for 3½" (9 cm). Change to size 5 (3.75 mm) needles and work in St st until piece measures 26½ (27½, 28½)" (67.5 [70, 72.5] cm).

Next row: Work 17 (25, 32) sts in St st, work center 66 sts in seed st, work rem 17 (25, 32) sts in St st. Repeat until piece measures 30 (31, 32)" (76 [78.5, 81] cm). BO in pat sts.

Left Front

With size 4 (3.5 mm) needles, CO 80 (96, 110) sts. Work in seed st for 3½" (9 cm), slipping first st of every WS row. Change to size 5 (3.75 mm) needles. Next row (RS): K65 (81, 95), place marker, work remaining 15 sts in seed st as set. Next row (WS): Slip 1, work 14 sts in seed st, slip marker, p65 (81, 95). Repeat last 2 rows (slipping marker on all subsequent rows, and working in St st with 15 edge sts in seed st, continuing to slip first st of WS rows) until piece measures 13" (33 cm), ending with a WS row. Begin edge shaping: K to 2 sts before marker, k2tog, work rem 15 sts in seed st as set. Work 3 rows even. Repeat these 4 rows 19 times more, then work dec row every other row 28 (36, 43) times. Work even until piece measures same as back. BO in pat sts.

Right Front

Work as for Left Front, reversing all shaping.

Sleeves

With size 4 (3.5 mm) needles, CO 75 (85, 95) sts. Work in seed st for 3½" (9 cm). Change to size 5 (3.75 mm) needles and work in St st, inc 1 st at each end every 10 rows 5 times—85 (95, 105) sts. Work even until piece measures 10" (25.5 cm). BO.

Ties

Left Tie: CO 15 sts. Slipping the first st of each row, work in seed st for 34" (86.5 cm). Bind off in pat. Right Tie: CO 15 sts. Slipping the first st of each row, work in seed st for 12" (30.5 cm). Bind off in pat.

Finishing

Sew shoulder seams. Sew sleeves to body. Sew side and sleeve seams. Sew Right Tie to Right Front edge at the point where shaping begins. Sew 12" (30.5 cm) piece of seam binding to corresponding point on Left Front edge. Sew Left Tie to corresponding point on outside of left side seam. Sew 12" (30.5 cm) piece of seam binding to corresponding point on inside of right side seam.

The seed stitch wraps all the way around the back, a veritable cocoon of the stitch pattern we adore for its good behavior and lack of curling at the edge.

Cotton chenille is a delicious choice for a washcloth: there's nothing softer, and its velvety texture makes the pattern blur in an interesting way.

DISHCLOTH RELOADED

Quick! We've gone ten pages without a dishcloth pattern! We cannot quite get enough of dishcloths, especially ones with a lot of features: bobbles, yarn overs, decreases down to nothingness. Our online friend Brooks Jones sent us this pattern. It was like getting a casserole in our e-mail box. Never mind a star on the sidewalk in Hollywood; true fame is having a dishcloth pattern named for you.

When you have had enough of the rectangle, the square, the trapezoid dishcloth, Brooks's deluxe version is a postgraduate-level dishcloth that gives a person a lot to think about.

MASON-DIXON WASHCLOTH

By Brooks Jones

This charming washcloth is knit in the round from the outside in. The most challenging bits are in the first few rows, when you will experience the thrill of making bobbles *and* eyelets while keeping your decreases even. If you can do this bit and watch TV at the same time, be sure to shout out, "Day-um, I'm *good!*"

SIZE: Approx 11" (28 cm) diameter from bobble to bobble

MATERIALS: Peaches & Creme worsted weight by Elmore-Pisgah Inc., [solid colors 2½ oz (71.5 g) balls, each approx 122 yds (112 m); cotton] 1 ball in pale green or Cotton Chenille by Crystal Palace Yarns [1¾ oz (50 g) hanks, each approx 98 yds (108 m)] 1 ball in chartreuse

Size 8 (5 mm) circular needle

One set (5) size 8 (5 mm) double-pointed needles

GAUGE: 18 sts + 26 rows = 4" (10 cm) over St st.

**Special Abbreviation
mb (make bobble)**

K into the back, front and back of next stitch, turn, p3, turn, k3, turn, p3, turn, sl 1, k2tog, pass the slipped stitch over.

Note: You will be starting at the outside edge and knitting into the center, decreasing as you go. Using circular needle and leaving a longer-than-usual cast-on tail, CO 150 sts.

ROUND 1: Purl.

ROUND 2: [K12, mb, k12] 6 times.

ROUND 3: Purl.

ROUND 4: [K10, ssk, k1, k2tog, k10] 6 times. (138 sts).

ROUND 5 (Eyelet Round): {[K1, yo, k2tog] 3 times, k4, [k1, yo, k2tog] 3 times, k1} 6 times.

ROUND 6: [K9, ssk, k1, k2tog, k9] 6 times. (126 sts).

ROUND 7 AND FOLLOWING ALTERNATE ROUNDS: Knit.

ROUND 8: [K8, ssk, k1, k2tog, k8] 6 times (114 sts).

ROUND 10: [K7, ssk, k1, k2tog, k7] 6 times (102 sts).

ROUND 12: [K6, ssk, k1, k2tog, k6] 6 times (90 sts).

ROUND 14: [K5, ssk, k1, k2tog, k5] 6 times (78 sts).

ROUND 16: [K4, ssk, k1, k2tog, k4] 6 times (66 sts).

Switch to double-pointed needles here or thereabouts.

ROUND 18: [K3, ssk, k1, k2tog, k3] 6 times (54 sts).

ROUND 20: [K2, ssk, k1, k2tog, k2] 6 times. (42 sts)

ROUND 22: [K1, ssk, k1, k2tog, k1] 6 times. (30 sts)

ROUND 24: [Ssk, k1, k2tog] 6 times. (18 sts)

ROUND 26: [Sl 1, k2tog, psso] 6 times. (6 sts)

Draw yarn through remaining 6 sts to fasten off.

Optional Hanging Loop

Using cast-on tail and size J/10 (6 mm) crochet hook, ch 12. Attach end of chain to other side of bobble and sew down. Weave in ends. Pin into a hexagonal shape on flat surface and use water mister to block lightly. Allow to dry completely.

Hey, Michael Graves, what your postmodern teakettle needs is a Mason-Dixon dishcloth on its handle!

Square yet not really square: we love the irregular edges of these boxes when they nest together.

I have a very *strong urge* to knit all the furniture.

Kay

CONTAINERS FOR YOUR JOY: FELTED BOXES

I am convinced that I got my irresistible urge to stash materials from my Grandpa Gardiner, who was a stone mason for more than fifty years. He retired at the age of sixty-five (he had started at twelve), but most mornings still found him at "the mill," hanging out with bricklayers and sorting through scraps of granite, sandstone, and marble. He'd bring them back to his tiny hip-roofed garage. I cannot remember what the garage looked like inside, because I never saw it except through a haze of stone dust, with my fingers in my ears to muffle the scream of the saw.

Like me with my odd balls of yarn, Grandpa used his stone stash to make wacky and exquisite objects of his own design. Since he no longer had any banks or civic buildings to embellish and fortify, he embellished and fortified our two small bungalows and their adjoining yards.

Naturally, the walls of our driveway and all our walks were lined with artfully chiseled stone walls. We had a stone bench and Grandpa's granite-clad porch had lovely marble pedestals for flowerpots. William Randolph Hearst's castle at San Simeon could not have a garbage can enclosure as nice as the one in our back alley. Surrounding things with stone came naturally to Grandpa. He wandered around with a bucket of mortar, and he always had a trowel in his pocket.

I do the same as Grandpa, only with knitting. I have a very strong urge to knit all the furniture. One of the things I have most wished for is a knitted storage container. The mail-order catalog people have overdone the wicker shelf basket, and I don't like the way wicker can scratch wooden surfaces, or snag on upholstery (and knitting). Felted bowls and bags make excellent storage, but I wanted a rectilinear container—for a modern look, but also so I could fit several together on a shelf or under the bench by the door, and easily see what's inside. I dreamed of large, felted boxes. How beautiful and practical they would be, holding keys, mittens, and overdue library books by the door, or DVDs and old passports on a bookshelf. A felted box seemed like such a snap to knit that I wondered why I didn't see them everywhere.

My first, oh, dozen efforts met with failure. No matter how I tried, my boxes always wanted to poof out on the sides into a shallow bowl shape. Despite felting and re-felting, the walls were too thin to stand up on their own, or contain the contents. Even the best of my felted box prototypes were not giving the wicker shelf basket a run for its money.

I was about to give up, defeated by the simple felted box, when I hit upon the idea of double-stranding bulky yarn, and making a "fold line" at the bottom edges of the box, which helped the sides stop bulging out. Now I was off to the races. I bought many (MANY!) more skeins of Lamb's Pride Bulky, and set to work. The result is this set of nesting Felted Boxes. They remind me of a set of 1950s bowls in Pyrex or melamine. I like the way the handles on all four sides make them resemble mini–milk crates. I like the knife-edge corners, and I like the corrugated-cardboard texture, which comes from garter stitch. Very boxlike. Very practical. Grandpa would approve.

TECHNICAL HINTS

Oh, No! Creases in My Felted Box! Help! ★ **The centrifugal force of the spin cycle, or a crowded washer, can cause creases in your felted box. You can avoid these creases entirely by removing the box before the final spin, but a sopping wet box takes much longer to dry.**

Usually you can avoid creases by removing the item immediately after the spin cycle ends, and promptly shaping and steaming it. You can remove creases by wetting with a spray bottle and steaming heavily.

Felting in Front-loading Washers ★ **I have better success felting in a top-loading machine with an agitator, but by necessity I sometimes felt in a front-loader. It just takes a bit of bravery to felt "blind" (you can't check on your felting mid-cycle when there is water in the machine). To deal with any creases that may form in the final spin, see the tip about creases.**

The secret: doubling the yarns. Doubled yarns make for the sturdiest kind of felt.

FELTED BOXES

Making these vibrant, chunky boxes is quick and addicting. I made six of them the first week, and I keep finding more uses for them. I stash all my bits and bobs in them. Mostly, I rearrange them on the bookshelves, feeling pleased with myself.

SIZE: Small (Medium, Large). The small box is 5½" x 6" x 4" (14 cm x 15 cm x 10 cm), the medium box is 7½" x 8" x 4½" (19 cm x 20 cm x 11 cm), and the large box is 9" x 9½" x 5" (23 cm x 24 cm x 12 cm).

MATERIALS: Lamb's Pride Bulky by Brown Sheep, [4 oz (112 g) skeins, each approx 125 yds (114 m), wool/mohair] 2 (3, 3) skeins in any color or combination of colors. I cannot stand to miss an opportunity to change colors, so I never used more than one skein of a single color in any of my boxes.

Size 10 (6 mm) needles or size needed to achieve gauge

Size J/10 (6 mm) crochet hook (exact size not important, but it must be large enough to work with a single strand of the yarn)

GAUGE: 12 sts + 12 garter ridges = 4" (10 cm) over garter st (before felting). Notes: The yarn is used doubled throughout the pattern. The right side ("RS") forms the inside of the box.

Side One

CO 12 (16, 20) sts. Working in garter stitch, knit 4 ridges.

Make handle: On the next row (RS), k4 (5, 6), BO 4 (6, 8), k4 (5,6). On the next row (WS), k4 (5, 6), CO 4 (6, 8), k4 (5, 6).

Knit 6 (7, 8) garter ridges and knit the next row.

Make first folding seam: On the next row (WS), purl.

Bottom

Knit 12 (16, 20) garter ridges and knit the next row. Make second folding seam: On the next row (WS), purl.

Side Two

Knit 6 (7, 8) garter ridges.

Make handle: On the next row (RS), k4 (5, 6), BO 4 (6, 8), k4 (5,6). On the next row (WS), k4 (5, 6), CO 4 (6, 8), k4 (5, 6). Knit 3 garter ridges. BO all sts.

Side Three

WS (outside of box) facing, pick up and k12 (16, 20) sts. Knit the next (RS) row. Make folding seam: On the next row (WS), purl. Knit 6 (7, 8) garter ridges.

Make handle: On the next row (RS), k4 (5, 6), BO 4 (6, 8), k4 (5,6). On the next

Joining the box corners

1 **Make a slip knot. Insert hook into 1 row on each side at the bottom of box and pull a loop of yarn through both stitches. Now you have 2 loops on the hook.**

row (WS), k4 (5, 6), CO 4 (6, 8), k4
(5, 6). Knit 3 garter ridges (6 rows).
BO all sts.

Side Four

Same as side three.

Finishing

Fold up the sides of the box and, using
a single strand of the yarn, single-crochet
each corner together on the outside of
box. Sew in ends and trim short.

Felting

Place in washing machine filled to the
lowest water level with hot water. Add a
small amount of detergent or liquid soap
and a pair of old jeans. Let the washer run
through its wash cycle using a cold rinse.

Shape the box, placing it upright on a flat
surface. Fill the box with rolled-up washcloths or small towels, which will help it

dry by absorbing water from the inside of
the box. Steam the box to set its shape,
and let it set until it is completely dry.

For less fuzz, use a disposable razor to
shave the outside of the box. (*Free*

Relationship Advice: If you don't have a
disposable one handy, be careful whose
razor you use. Most men have a mortal
fear of any woman borrowing their
razor, for any reason.)

> ## TECHNICAL HINTS
>
> **Nesting Boxes That Really Nest** ★ **If you are making a set of nesting boxes, be sure to felt all three boxes at the same time. Felting is a somewhat unpredictable process—remember, the wool you are using probably does not all come from the same sheep. By felting your boxes in the same load, you can at least control the variables associated with the washing machine.**
>
> **It Never Hurts to Ask** ★ **You probably know that wool that is labeled "Super Wash" has been treated so that it will not shrink, which means that it will not felt, which means that you shouldn't try to make a felted box out of it. But did you also know that some untreated wools do not felt well? If you're unsure about a brand or color, ask before you buy.**

with single crochet:

Fold up 2 adjoining sides of the box, with wrong sides together. Do
not fret about the appearance of your crochet; the single strand of
yarn is invisible after felting.

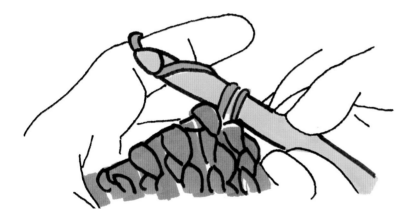

2 Pull another loop of yarn through
both loops on the hook, leaving you with
a single loop.

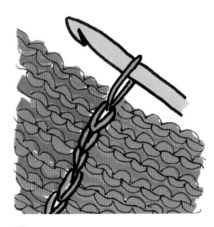

3 Repeat steps 1 and 2 all the way
up to the top of the box. The edges
should match perfectly because
each side of the box has the same
number of rows.

Chapter Three

LOG CABIN KNITTING

GIVE ME LAND, LOTS OF LAND—COVERED IN

GARTER STITCH.

How did I get here?

WHY IS THE SQUARE SO COMPELLING?

Kay ✳ I am an ardent knitter of Square Stuff. I love to knit all manner of rectilinear shapes, from cushions and bags to bedspreads. Yes, bedspreads, dammit. I have given serious thought to knitting a hammock and a shower curtain, and at any given moment I have a beach blanket in progress. I am no stranger to rugs and mats, and the idea of cranking out some wall-to-wall carpet sounds pretty interesting to me. Give me land, lots of land—covered in garter stitch. How did I get here? Why is the square so compelling?

THE TROUBLE WITH SWEATERS

Part of it has to do with wanting a less complicated but more creative knitting experience. Several years ago, I realized that I was a pattern knitter, but not just any pattern knitter. The case was quite serious: I was a serial Rowan pattern knitter. Every six months, the new Rowan magazine would arrive, and I would fall in love with the season's new yarns and designs. Maybe it's my Northern European DNA, but I felt a kinship with the pale, languid young women modeling the sweaters. (Hey, I'm pale. I'm languid.) Before long, the Rowanettes would start talking up one of the designs on the Knitting Circle chat board, and all of a sudden I'd be caught up in mass Anglophiliac knitting hysteria. I felt sure that if I just set my mind to it, I could soon be leaning against a dappled stone wall—wearing slingbacks, a swingy skirt, and my very own Kaffe Fassett miracle, Smolder—waiting for my cute boyfriend.

As it turns out, however, a sweater does not look exactly the same on a fortysomething mother of two as it does on the leggy twenty-year-old model who is wearing the sweater (and, often, only the sweater) while cavorting on the moody, misty moors of Yorkshire. I have found that I can put on a Rowan cardigan and sit at a sidewalk café for hours without encountering even one dangerously handsome guy (also wearing a fab Rowan handknit), who wants to buy me a cocktail.

Maybe I just haven't waited long enough.

There were other problems besides sweater disappointment. I did not always have the energy to do all the fiddling and figuring that goes into making a sweater. Sometimes, I just wanted to knit without the stop-and-start of shaping, in an easy-to-memorize pattern. I wanted something I could knit without looking away from a riveting British drama on PBS. I simply cannot give proper attention to the travails of the dashing Inspector Lynley (rawr!) while counting the rows between side-shaping increases.

THE ONE TRUE FAITH:
LOG CABIN KNITTING

The moment that really changed my knitting life was when I found log cabin knitting. In truth, log cabin knitting found me. I was cruising through the "Finished Objects" featured on an online photo album for Rowanettes, and stopped dead in my tracks at a baby blanket made by Jill Richards. The blanket was in every color of Rowan Handknit Cotton that Jill had lying around the house (which

means a lot of colors, because Jill can turn out cotton sweaters like nobody's business, and she has been doing it for decades). Jill's blanket vibrated with visual energy. It glowed with rich color. But what was most striking was the blanket's construction: Jill had started with a small center patch, picked up stitches and knitted strips all around this center patch, then picked up and knitted strips around those strips, each strip slightly longer than the strip beneath it. It had a simplicity and vibrancy that reminded me of Amish quilts. It was homey and folksy, but fresh and modern at the same time.

The technique that Jill used mimics the traditional log cabin pattern used in quilt-making, in which strips of fabric are pieced around a central patch to form concentric squares. Quilters know endless variations on the log cabin theme. There are versions called "Housetop" and "Bricklayer," in which the the strips are arranged to create striking pyramid shapes, and "Sunshine and Shadow," which boldly contrasts light and dark. Contemporary quilters do jazzy riffs in which log cabin strips go tilting off in all directions. A quilter (or knitter) who has an inventive eye can tweak the "rules" of the traditional log cabin, but it remains recognizable as a log cabin. Like all good rules, the log cabin rules are meant to be broken.

Can you get vertigo from a blanket? Ann Buechner made this wildly tilting log cabin using instructions by Woolly Thoughts. The Woolly Thoughts website offers a mind-blowing array of knitting designs based on mathematical principles. (*www.woollythoughts.com*)

HOW TO LOG CABIN

Start with the center patch.

1. Cast on 20 stitches, knit 24 garter ridges, then bind off on the right side.

One rule throughout: Always bind off on a right side row, leaving one stitch in the upper left corner of your patch, as shown.

Pick up stitches for the first strip.

With the right side of the center patch facing you, turn the patch clockwise, so that the top of the piece has the single stitch on the far right, and the row ends along the top. Pick up one stitch in each garter ridge. (You will have 24 stitches, but the beauty of log cabin knitting is that you don't have to count stitches.)

2. Now make the first strip. Knit 9 garter ridges, and then bind off on a right side row and turn the work to the right.

Pick up for the second strip.

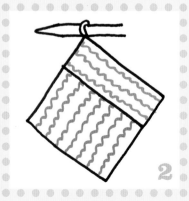

The interesting thing here is that you first pick up stitches from the ends of the 9 garter ridges of the strip you just finished, and then you continue picking up across the cast-on edge of the center patch. When picking up stitches, always pick up one stitch for every stitch on the cast-on or bound-off edge.

3. Now knit the second strip. Knit 9 garter ridges, bind off on the right side, and turn the work clockwise.

Pick up for the third strip.

4. Knit the third strip. Like the previous strips, knit 9 garter ridges, bind off on the right side, and turn the work clockwise.

Enclose the center patch with a fourth strip.

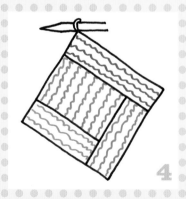

5. To complete the enclosure of the center patch, pick up stitches from the 9 garter ridges of the third strip, then from the bound-off edge of the center patch, and finally from the 9 garter ridges of first strip. Not that we need to count, but this should be 38 stitches in all. Knit 9 garter ridges, bind off on the right side, and turn the work clockwise.

From here, it's clear sailing, nothing but Zen, Zen, Zen. Every time you finish a strip, you do the same things:

1. Turn the work to the right.

2. Pick up stitches from the garter ridges.

3. Pick up stitches along the bound-off edge of the adjoining strip.

4. Pick up from the garter ridges of the adjoining strip.

5. Knit a new strip and bind off all stitches except the last stitch.

6. Rinse and repeat!

Keep at it until you run out of colors, or yarn, or energy, or surfaces to cover with glorious log cabin textiles. Put a border on it, or not. Give it to somebody you love.

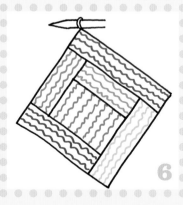

TECHNICAL HINTS

What is a garter ridge? ★ Garter stitch is formed by knitting every row on both sides of the work. When you knit a row on the RS, the "purl bumps" show on the WS; conversely when you knit a row on the WS, the "purl bumps" form a "garter ridge" on the RS of the knitted fabric. Each garter ridge is formed from two rows of knitting. When knitting and designing log cabin patterns, it is easier to count the garter ridges than the rows.

For "Joseph's Blankie of Many Colors," all the stitches are picked up on the right side of the work, giving the appearance of a smooth, invisible seam. Picking up stitches on the wrong side gives the effect of ticking fabric, in which a dotted line of the new color appears on the right side.

The first time I did this (by accident, of course), I thought: Crikey—that looks just like a quilt! Picking up stitches from the wrong side creates a "flaw" that attracts the eye and highlights the pattern's rhythm.

JOSEPH'S BLANKIE OF MANY COLORS

SIZE: 47" x 47" (120 cm x 120 cm)

MATERIALS: Cotton Classic by Tahki Yarns/Tahki-Stacy Charles, Inc., [1 ¾ oz (50 g), 108 yds (100 m), mercerized cotton] 24 colors, 2 hanks of each color, plus one hank in a different color for the center patch.

Size 6 (4mm) needles

GAUGE: 20 sts + 40 rows = 4" (10 cm) in garter stitch.

Note: The colors are not specified, leaving you free to choose your own color design. If you wish to replicate the blanket in the picture, use "warm" colors (reds, yellows, pinks and oranges) for one right angle of the log cabin square, and "cool" colors (blues, greens, and lavender) for the other angle.

CO 20 sts for the center patch, and knit 24 garter ridges. Then follow the basic log cabin instructions on page 68, using the chart above to determine the number and placement of strips, each of which has garter ridges.

Make a border as described on page 75.

FREE AT LAST

In knitting as in quilting, log cabin blankets are constructed by "piecing" strips together. It would be possible to replicate a log cabin design by using the intarsia method: starting at the bottom of the blanket and knitting the colors in, row by row, following a chart. But why do that when it is so much fun to knit log cabin strips, and you only have to deal with one color of yarn at a time?

Once I got the knack of log cabin, I discovered I could do it any old way that looked good to me. My log cabins can be square or rectangular. I can get down with my inner artiste and stick in a short row here or there, which makes the strips lopsided or even triangular. I can use the log cabin method to make knitted tributes to fabric quilts that I admire, or I can dream up an asymmetrical grid that looks like something Piet Mondrian would have knitted, if he hadn't been so busy with the oil paints.

The best part is that whenever I'm knitting log cabins, I'm having a blast. It's pure play. No counting stitches. No increasing, no decreasing, no am-I-supposed-to-knit-this-stitch-on-the-wrong-side-and-purl-it-on-the-right-side? Any time I need a break from something else, I can pick up my log cabin project (I've always got one going) and experience calm and fun. Zen. God's in His heaven and all's right with the world.

With log cabin knitting, we don't need no stinkin' patterns. With vision and our feet on the ground, we can be artists, in the spirit of the Shakers or the quilters of Gee's Bend. The icing on the cake is that our grandkids will fight over the blankets.

For one of her first knitting projects, Pamela Hubbard made a mini-version of Joseph's Blankie. Pam's only trouble was that everybody who saw her working on it asked her to make one for them.

THE IMPORTANCE OF BEING BLANKETED

It is not only the easy freedom of knitting blankets that draws me to them. A handknit blanket is an honest-to-goodness heirloom. It is a symbol of warmth and love. If it's a beautiful blanket, it's going to be around long after a handknit sweater has given out at the elbows or been outgrown. It is not going too far, I think, to say that a handknit blanket is a form of immortality.

And if it's adopted by a child, a blanket need not be beautiful, and it need not be in good shape. It needn't even be all that clean. It needs only to keep existing. A nasty old shred of a blanket can call back moments of sweet-smelling comfort. If you knit a blanket for your boy, there is a good chance that, long after he stops submitting to homemade sweaters, the blanket will go with him, to a dorm room or maybe even to his first apartment. (Let's try not to think about the make-out possibilities that a handknit blanket can afford.)

WORKING IT YOUR WAY

Once you understand the mechanics of log cabin knitting, you can start to play with it. Your log cabin will have a very different look if, instead of continually turning the work clockwise, after you have finished the first strip, you go to the opposite side of the work and knit a strip there. If you keep knitting mirrored pairs of strips on opposite sides of the center patch, you will create a log cabin square or rectangle that looks like four triangles or pyramids around the center patch.

If the colors of the pyramids contrast, wow. Very graphic, and très moderne. In quilting, this arrangement of log cabin strips is called "Courthouse Steps." The Gee's Bend quilters call it "Bricklayer," and when I'm knitting one I get the workmanlike satisfaction that I imagine my stonemason grandpa got from making a brick wall perfectly level. No matter what this pattern is called, making it feeds the soul. I can't explain it. Try it and see.

A handknit blanket is an honest-to-goodness *heirloom.*

Whether you call it
Courthouse Steps or
Bricklayer, this slight tweak
to the basic Log Cabin
recipe has a dramatic effect.

It is a symbol of warmth and love.

COURTHOUSE STEPS DENIM BLANKET

This design is a knitted tribute to one of the Gee's Bend quilts, "Bricklayer," by Loretta Pettway, which I was lucky enough to see at an exhibition at the Whitney Museum of American Art in 2003. I stood in front of that quilt for a long time, thinking about how Loretta Pettway had transformed threadbare workclothes into such a bold and moving work of art. Because the original quilt is made of well-worn denim pants, my version uses a denim yarn that shrinks and fades in the first wash, and continues to fade gently with use and subsequent washings. I washed my blanket many times while making it, throwing it in with a load of jeans after each round of strips was completed.

SIZE: 50" x 38" (127 cm x 100 cm)

MATERIALS: Denim by Rowan Yarns, [1¾ oz (50 g) balls, each approx 93 yds (85 m), cotton]
A: light blue 14 balls
B: dark indigo 8 balls
C: cream 4 balls
Size 6 (4mm) needles

GAUGE: 20 sts + 40 rows = 4" (10 cm) in garter stitch.

Start with a center patch, and then consult the chart to determine the placement and color of the strips.

Note: For each number on the chart, there are 2 mirrored strips on opposite sides of the blanket. You can knit either of these strips first, but you must knit both strips before you move on to the next number. On odd-numbered strips, stitches are always picked up from the WS. On even-numbered strips, stitches are always picked up from the RS.

Center Patch

Using A, CO 13 sts. Knit 23 garter ridges. BO on the RS. Begin following the chart. Strip 1: Using B, pick up 23 sts FROM THE WRONG SIDE in the garter ridges along one side of the center patch. Knit 9 garter ridges. BO on the RS. Next, on this strip and EVERY OTHER ODD-NUMBERED STRIP: Using C, pick up 23 sts FROM THE WRONG SIDE of the same strip. Knit 1 garter ridge and BO on the RS. Then repeat Strip 1 on the opposite edge of the center patch. STRIP 2: Using A, pick up 13 sts along the cast-on or bound-off edge of the center patch. Knit 9 garter ridges. BO on the RS. Continue following the chart until you have completed Strip 16 on both sides.

STRIP 17: Using B and FROM THE WRONG SIDE, pick up stitches in the garter ridges of Strip 16 and the bound-off edge of Strip 15. Knit 1 garter ridge and BO on the RS. Then, using C and FROM THE WRONG SIDE, pick up stitches in the stitches just bound off. Knit 9 garter ridges and BO on the RS. Repeat Strip 17 on the opposite side.

STRIP 18: Using A, pick up stitches in the garter ridges of Strip 17 and the bound-off edge of Strip 16. Knit 9 garter ridges and BO on the RS. Repeat Strip 18 on the opposite side.

Border

Using B, make a border as described on page 75.

Hoo boy, this is a shiny bath rug. It knits up quickly in a superchunky mercerized cotton. Plus, you get to sit out a trip to Bed Bath and Beyond Human Endurance.

SNAZZY BATH RUG

This chunky rug is a variation on the Courthouse Steps pattern, with the strips varying in width.

SIZE: 23" x 26.5" (59 cm x 67 cm)

MATERIALS: Weekend Cotton by Classic Elite, [3½ oz (100 g) balls, each approx 51 yds (46m) cotton]
A: variegated red/fuschia/orange multi, 3 hanks
B: red, 3 hanks
C: fuschia, 3 hanks
Size 10½ (6.5 mm) needles

GAUGE: 11 sts x 22 rows = 4" (10 cm) in garter stitch.

Note: For each strip number indicated below, you will knit 2 mirrored strips on opposite sides of the rug. (You can knit either of these strips first, but you must knit both strips before you move on to the next number.)

Center patch

Using B, CO 23 sts. Knit 23 garter ridges. BO on the RS.

STRIP 1: Using A, pick up 23 sts in the garter ridges along one side of the center patch. Knit 8 garter ridges. BO on the RS. Repeat Strip 1 on the opposite edge of the center patch.

STRIP 2: Using C, pick up 39 sts along the row ends of Strip 1 and the cast-on or bound-off edge of the center patch.

Knit 12 garter ridges. BO on the RS. Repeat on the opposite side.

STRIP 3: Using A, pick up 47 sts in the row ends of Strip 2 and the cast-on or bound-off edge of Strip 1. Knit 8 garter ridges. BO on the RS. Repeat on the opposite side.

STRIP 4: Using C, pick up 55 sts in the row ends of Strip 3 and the cast-on or bound-off edge of Strip 2. Knit 8 garter ridges. BO on the RS. Repeat on the opposite side.

Border

This rug has a mitered border that looks like a picture frame. Using a circular needle and B, pick up one stitch in each bound-off stitch FROM THE WRONG SIDE of one of the outer edges of the rug. Knit 4 garter ridges. At the same time, increase one stitch at each end of every RS row by knitting into the front and back of the first and last stitch. BO on the RS. Repeat on the remaining 3 edges. Join the border at the corners using mattress stitch.

Finishing

Using C, whipstitch around the bound-off edge of the border. Dampen the rug, shape it, and allow to dry.

MUST-KNIT TV

★ ★ ★ ★ ★ ★ ★ ★ ★

Knitting and TV were made for each other. Neither requires full attention at all times. But not every TV show is primo knitting TV. Our field-tested favorites:

ANN:

👁 *The Daily Show with Jon Stewart*

👁 *Take Me Home: The John Denver Story*

👁 local Stormtracker 2000 radar coverage of violent weather systems

KAY:

👁 All Things BBC: mystery, Britcom, soap, anything reminiscent of Yorkshire (including Miss Marple if she's desperate)

👁 *Antiques Roadshow U.K.*

ANN AND KAY:

👁 *Frontier House*

👁 *Manor House*

👁 *Colonial House*

👁 *Regency House Party*

👁 *This Old House*

👁 *Bleak House*

ANY MARRIED WOMAN:

Husband's action movies. Kay has sat through *The Hunt for Red October* enough times to knit several ponchos, but still has no clue what it is about or why the captain of the Soviet nuclear submarine has a Scottish burr.

ALL HELL BREAKS LOOSE

For adventurous types who want to go beyond blankets that look like traditional quilt patterns, the log cabin technique is a handy tool for free-form design. Get this: You do not need a "center patch." You do not need "strips." You knit a shape. It can be square, rectangular, triangular, or even curved. You bind off this piece. Then, you knit another shape onto it, by picking up stitches along an edge of the first piece. Piece by piece, you can create a blanket, a rug, a tea cozy, or a Very Interesting Textile. Others have pieced together sweaters using this method. No doubt that is a lot of fun, but it results in a very boxy sweater to my way of thinking. I, for one, am sticking to Square Stuff.

Where is it written that a baby blanket has to be babyish? It is never too early to impart good taste to the young. This blanket can stay with a kid, without embarrassment, all the way to adulthood.

This Moderne Log Cabin is as far from the countryside as a log cabin can get. Even we are amazed at the sleek feel of this throw, which would be at home in any penthouse boudoir.

MODERNE LOG CABIN BLANKET

This lightweight blanket in a sophisti-
cated wool/silk yarn proves that a log
cabin can go to the Big City. There is no
"center patch," and there are blocks of
color instead of concentric strips.
Drape it over a Barcelona chair, or your
shoulders, and enjoy.

SIZE: 60" x 50" (150 cm x 124 cm)

MATERIALS: Silky Wool by Elsebeth
Lavold, [1.76 oz (50 g) balls, each
approx 192 yds (176 m), wool/silk]
A: cream 4 balls
B: brown 5 balls

C: light purple 5 balls
D: dark purple 5 balls
Size 6 (4mm) needles

GAUGE: 22 sts + 44 rows = 4" (10 cm) in
garter stitch.

Note: Throughout pattern, always pick
up and bind off stitches on the RS.

BLOCK 1: Using A, CO 76 sts. Knit 66
garter ridges. BO.

BLOCK 2: Using B, pick up 66 sts from
the row ends along the right selvedge of
Block 1. Note: Pick up one st from each

row end. Knit 33 garter ridges. BO.

BLOCK 3: Using C, pick up 109 sts from
row ends of Block 2 and bound-off edge
of Block 1. Knit 66 garter ridges. BO.

BLOCK 4: Using D, pick up 132 sts along
bound-off edge of Block 2 and row ends
of Block 3. Knit 66 garter ridges. BO.

BLOCK 5: Using B, pick up 175 sts along
row ends of Block 4 and bound-off edge
of Block 3. Knit 33 garter ridges. BO.

BLOCK 6: Using B, pick up 165 sts along
bound-off edge of Block 4 and row ends
of Block 5. Knit 33 garter ridges. BO.

BLOCK 7: Using C, pick up 208 sts
along row ends of Block 6 and bound-
off edge of Block 5. Knit 66 garter
ridges. BO.

BLOCK 8: Using A, pick up 231 sts along
cast-off edge of Block 6 and row ends of
Block 7. Knit 66 garter ridges. BO.

BLOCK 9: See diagram. This block
creates two rectangles side by side. Use
the intarsia technique of lifting one color
over the other when changing colors, to
avoid a hole where the colors change.

Turn work so that the edge containing
Blocks 1, 2, 4, 6, and 8 is at top, RS
facing. Count 33 row ends of Block 4
and place marker at this center point of
Block 4. You will be picking up along
cast-on edge of Block 1 and row ends of
Blocks 2, 4, 6, and 8. Using B, pick up
142 sts to marker. Join D and pick up
132 sts . Knit 99 garter ridges, lifting one
color over the other when changing
colors. BO.

Border
Using D, make border as instructed on
page 75.

Finishing
Sew in all ends on the back of the work.
Lightly press with steam.

MODERNE BABY BLANKET

This is a crib-sized, easy-care version of the Moderne Log Cabin Blanket, for the modern baby.

SIZE: 38" x 28" (98 cm x 70 cm)

MATERIALS: Calmer by Rowan Yarns, [1¾ oz (50 g) balls, each approx 175 yds (160 m), cotton/acrylic/microfiber]
A: cream 3 balls
B: celery green 3 balls
C: sage green 3 balls
D: teal 3 balls
Size 6 (4 mm) needles

GAUGE: 21 sts + 42 rows = 4" (10 cm) in garter stitch.

Note: Throughout pattern, always pick up and bind off stitches on the RS.

BLOCK 1: Using A, CO 42 sts. Knit 36 garter ridges. BO.

BLOCK 2: Using B, pick up 36 sts from the row ends along the right selvedge of Block 1. Note: Pick up one stitch from each row end. Knit 18 garter ridges. BO.

BLOCK 3: Using C, pick up 60 stitches from row ends of Block 2 and bound-off edge of Block 1. Knit 36 garter ridges. BO.

BLOCK 4: Using D, pick up 72 stitches along bound-off edge of Block 2 and row ends of Block 3. Knit 36 garter ridges. BO.

BLOCK 5: Using A, pick up 96 stitches sts row ends of Block 4 and bound-off edge of Block 3. Knit 18 garter ridges. BO.

BLOCK 6: Using A, pick up 90 sts along bound-off edge of Block 4 and row ends of Block 5. K 18 garter ridges. BO.

BLOCK 7: Using B, pick up 114 sts along row ends of Block 6 and bound-off edge of Block 5. Knit 36 garter ridges. BO.

BLOCK 8: Using C, pick up 126 sts along bound-off edge of Block 6 and row ends of Block 7. Knit 36 garter ridges. BO.

BLOCK 9: (Note: See diagram. This block creates two squares side by side. Use the intarsia technique of lifting one color over the other when changing colors, to avoid a hole where the colors change.)

Turn work so that the edge containing Blocks 1, 3, 5, and 7 is at top, RS facing. Place marker 63 garter ridges from the edge. Using D, pick up 54 sts along row ends, starting at Block 7 and ending at the marker. Joining B, pick up 54 sts along row ends to end (108 sts). Keeping colors consistent, K 54 garter ridges. BO.

BLOCK 10: Turn work so that the edge containing Blocks 1, 2, 4, 6 and 8 is at top, RS facing. Place marker between Block 4 and Block 6. Using C, pick up 150 sts along row ends of Block 9, cast-on edge of Block 1, and row ends of Blocks 2 and 4, ending at the marker. Joining D, pick up 54 sts along row ends of Blocks 6 and 8. Keeping colors consistent, Knit 18 garter ridges. BO.

Border

Using A, make border as instructed on page 75.

Finishing

Sew in all ends on the back of the work. Lightly press with steam.

TAILGATE RAG RUG

One of our favorite games is See How Few Ends You Have to Weave In. This pattern makes a strip of two log cabin squares. It uses only one very long piece of yarn and a bunch of short strips of rags. Lots of rag ends (worth it!) but only two yarn ends (a relief!).

SIZE: This pattern makes a 12" x 24" (30 cm x 61 cm) block. Combine as many blocks as you like. The illustrated rug takes 3 blocks and is 24" x 48" (60 cm x 121 cm).

MATERIALS:

A: Peaches & Creme double worsted, [16 oz (.45 kg) cone, 400 yds (365 m) cotton], 4 cones

B: Rag balls, aka 1"-wide rag strips. Use all one color, or vary them as you like. Size 10½ (6.5 mm) needles

GAUGE: 11 sts + 20 rows = 4" (10 cm) in garter stitch.

Note: A is held double throughout. Do not cut A until the end of Strip 9.

STRIP 1: Using A, CO 17 stitches. Knit 14 garter ridges. BO on RS, leaving last stitch on right needle. Do not cut yarn.

STRIP 2: Turn work 90° to right, so that left edge of knitting is now at the top. Join B. Pick up stitches along edge beginning with stitch already on right

needle. To pick up, insert needle into horizontal strand between garter ridge bumps (16 sts). Knit 1 row using B. Cut B, leaving tail to be woven in later. Using A, knit 6 garter ridges. BO on right side, leaving final stitch on needle.

STRIP 3: Turn work 90° to right. Join B. Pick up stitches along edge of Strip 2

and cast-on edge of Strip 1. Knit 1 row using B. Cut B, leaving tail to be woven in later. Using A, knit 6 garter ridges. BO on right side, leaving final stitch on needle.

STRIP 4: Turn work 90° to right. Join B. Pick up stitches along edge of Strip 3 and righ selvedge edge of Strip 1. Cut B, leaving tail to be woven in later. Using A, knit 6 garter ridges. BO on right side, leaving final stitch on needle.

STRIP 5: Turn work 90° to right. Join B. Pick up stitches along edge of Strips 4, 1 (cast-off edge), and 2. Cut B, leaving tail to be woven in later. Using A, knit 6 garter ridges. BO on right side, leaving final stitch on needle.

STRIPS 6–9: These four strips are knitted as stripes—no binding off at the end of each strip. Join B. Pick up stitches along edge of Blocks 5, 2, 3. Knit 1 row.

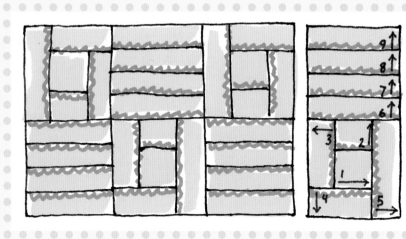

Cut B, leaving tail. Using A, knit 6 garter ridges. DO NOT BO. Repeat this strip three more times, then BO.

Make as many blocks as you like, then sew them together as shown in the illustration. Hell, go all out and make some wall-to-wall log cabin carpet.

Edging

An edging is optional, but we think it finishes the rug in a lurvly way. This superdeluxe edging involves a 60" (150 cm) circular needle, a large crochet hook, a will of iron, and two 6" (15 cm)-diameter rag balls. You create an edging around the rug one side at a time. Pick up stitches along one side of the rug, using a large crochet hook to pull the rag ball yarn through the edge of the rug. (The stitches are probably too tight to pick up stitches with the knitting needle.) Place stitches onto the circular needle. When you've reached the end of a side, do not cut the rag ball—you will continue picking up stitches on the next side of the rug. Slide the stitches you just picked up down the circular needle so that the stitches are now all on the left-hand side of the needle point—as if you're ready to knit with them. Beginning with the first stitch you picked up, BO each stitch, joining in a second rag ball. This makes a pretty chain edging. When you reach the end of side 1, do not cut rag ball number 2— you'll need it again in a minute. Just turn the corner. Going back to rag ball one, continue picking up stitches along side 2, and repeat the BO technique. When you get to the final corner, you'll have four ends to sew in. Or you can braid them in a short little tail.

POLO SHIRT PATCHWORK BLANKET

★ ★ ★ ★ ★ ★ ★ ★ ★ ★ ★ ★

Kay • Making knitted versions of quilts can lead to a whole new obsession: actual quilting. I never truly appreciated quilts until I tried to knit one. Now I concoct all kinds of schemes to get handmade quilts and blankets without learning how to sew. When you start saving old clothes, can patchwork be far off?

I've been hoarding my little boy's cotton piqué polo shirts for almost five years now. Joseph has been wearing piqué polo shirts since infancy. I didn't know what I was going to do with them, but by God, I was going to keep them. Joseph's dad is also a big consumer of piqué polo shirts. He is 6-foot-7 and of robust physique, so one of his shirts would back a baby blanket. You can see it coming, can't you? The Father-Son Polo Shirt Patchwork Blanket.

A sewing machine helps, but is not absolutely necessary. Treasured heirloom 100% guaranteed. (Hint: If the fronts are too yucky, use the backs.)

A neutral bathmat is the essence of pure 'n' simple, crunchy-granola log cabining. We used a strand each of cream, khaki, and tan held together. Neutral doesn't have to be boring.

ABSORBA, THE GREAT BATHMAT

Why the heck not? Why not hold three strands of double worsted Peaches & Creme together? It makes for the sort of mat that will absorb two or three gallons of bathwater.

SIZE: 18" x 27" (46 cm x 69 cm)

MATERIALS: Peaches & Creme double worsted [16 oz (.45 kg) cone, 400 yds (365 m) cotton], three cones of either complementary, contrasting, or identical colors.

Size 15 (10mm) needles or size needed to achieve gauge in garter st.

GAUGE: 9 sts + 17 rows = 4" (10 cm)

DIRECTIONS: Holding three strands of yarn together, CO 17 stitches. Knit 17 garter ridges. Using basic Log Cabin technique (page 62), make 9 strips around the center square, each having 6 garter ridges. To make mat rectangular, add a 10th strip to the side of the mat opposite Strip 9.

CRASHING ABOUT WITH A CREATIVE DERVISH: *Ann Hahn Buechner*

When we first heard from Ann Hahn Buechner, we were amazed at the way her one paragraph contained six ideas we immediately wanted to make. Ann's overflowing stream of projects inspires us all the time. Her Flying Geese blanket on page 79 takes the log cabin idea to a brand-new neighborhood. She is the poster child for Take an Idea and Run with It.

Q: Where does all this come from? You and the ideas—it's unbelievable how fertile your imagination is.

A: I read an interview with Julia Child a while back. The questions were all soft and fuzzy: "How do you get creative?" And Julia just blasted that down. She said she had to work hard for her ideas—and that meant having a good meal, a good night's sleep, then working hard at what she needed to solve/create/fix. I was so relieved to read that. Why not look at color/texture/design problems like they are buggy software or unbal-anced budgets or a floor that needs to be washed? I like that idea of using the right brain to help the left—or whichever way it is.

Q: What's on your bedside table?

A: My first knitting book was Barbara Walker's *Knitting from the Top.* It forces you to measure yourself or your model—and really think about the armhole depth, neckline, shape you want. My gauge loosens as I knit, and I really need to try things on as I go along to compensate for this familiarity. I like Anna Zilboorg's *Knitting for Anarchists* for this kind of advice and also Maggie Righetti's books [*Knitting in Plain English, Sweater Design in Plain English*]. They really go hand in hand with Elizabeth Zimmermann's advice. You should knit what you like, and not what you think you should be knitting. If a yarn doesn't feel good on the needles, switch needles or switch yarn—don't waste time working against yourself!

Q: What advice would you give to someone just learning to knit?

A: I find that people get too caught up in directions, and this keeps them from learning to "see" things for themselves. They'll say, "But the book says . . ." or "They switch to a blue color there . . ." and really they want to make the whole thing pink, shorter, and with beads on the end.

I think swatching yarns "to see what they want to become," as Maggie Righetti says, is so important, then washing them to see what you're going to get in the end so you're not disappointed.

Q: At one point you were knitting a slipcover for a giant canvas boat tote. It was a fantastic, totally crazy project.

A: I saw a Virginia Woolf quote somewhere that said, "Arrange whatever pieces come your way," and I've been trying to do that. Instead of rejecting things for what they are not, use them for something else. If the yarn's too much like string, macramé it! A couple weeks ago I crocheted a string bag for the oatmeal canister to hold our cookies. My Canadian hemp will never be a tank top—who am I kidding?—but now we'll have a couple of interesting string bags around to whip out at the farmers' market.

People need courage to follow their gut. What keeps catching your eye? What are you drawn to again and again? Get a small project to try it out, like those felted Fair Isle bags or table mats, sweaters for dolls and babies, wire bracelets. Why spend six weeks struggling when you could be having fun?

FLYING GEESE BLANKET

By Ann Hahn Buechner

This Flying Geese pattern kicks the notion of knitting a quilt up a notch. The pattern adds a new shape, the triangle, to your repertory, but you use the familiar Log Cabin technique of joining the pieces together by picking up stitches along an edge. In this design, Ann Buechner deftly combines the more complex geese shapes with simple blocks in a subtly variegated yarn. If you use contrasting shades of a self-striping yarn for the triangles of the geese motif, you'll create constantly shifting waves of color.

This blanket is pieced together in much the same way as a fabric quilt. The strips of triangles, or "geese," which are made separately, are the ideal small project to carry around with you.

The large squares are picked up and knitted onto the edges of the triangle

For this Flying Geese blanket, Ann Buechner used varied weights of wool: leftover bits of Jamieson's jumper weight wool yarn and Rowan's Yorkshire Tweed 4-ply in reds, browns, and greens. For the large garter stitch blocks, she used La Lana Wools Random Fines in a slightly variegated red. The pattern simplifies matters by using the same weight of wool throughout, and we hope it captures some of Ann's dazzling color play.

strips (fewer seams to sew!). The small corner squares are miters that are picked up from the ends of the triangle strips, eliminating even more seams.

Note: If you don't mind weaving in ends, you can cut the yarn every time you finish a triangle. If you want to simplify, you can carry the yarn not in use up the side of the triangle, as you do when making stripes. On the left small triangle, you will have to "purl up" the stitches (pick them up from the wrong side) to be able to carry up the yarn. You can also just cut the yarn and pick up stitches like a normal person.

SIZE: Approx 29" x 41" (74 cm x 105 cm)
MATERIALS: Harris Yarns with Rowan DK [1¾ oz (50 g) balls, each approx 123 yds (113 m), wool]
A: apple green (A), 2 balls
B: moss green, 2 balls
C: lobster red, 4 balls
D: tomato red, 2 balls
E: brown, 1 ball
Size 6 (4 mm) needles or size needed to achieve gauge.
GAUGE: 20 sts + 39 rows over garter st

Triangle Strips
(Make 17)

Triangle A

Using A, CO 15 sts.

ROW 1: K to last 2 sts, k2tog.

Repeat Row 1 until 3 sts remain. Make centered double decrease as follows: slip 2 sts as if to knit tog, insert left needle into front of slipped sts from the left side of the sts, and return the sts to left needle, k3tog tbl. BO.

Triangle B

Using B, with RS facing, pick up 11 sts evenly along one of the short edges of Triangle A.

ROW 1: K to last 2 sts, k2tog.

Repeat Row 1 until 3 sts remain. Make centered double decrease as for Triangle A. BO.

Repeat Triangle B on the opposite edge of Triangle A. You now have a rectangle composed of 3 triangles.

With RS facing and Triangle A pointing up, pick up 15 sts along the top edge of the rectangle, taking care to pick up the eighth stitch from the point of Triangle A.

Repeat the forgoing instructions until you have a strip that contains 6 flying geese rectangles.

Large Squares
(Make 6)

Using C, with RS of one triangle strip facing, pick up 47 sts along the edge of the strip that is shown on the chart for the block you are making. Knit 45 garter ridges. BO on the RS.

Assemble the Block

You now have 6 pieces composed of one strip of triangles and one large square. Attach a second triangle strip to each block, with the triangles pointing in the direction shown on the chart.

Small Corner Squares

In the bottom right corner of each block, there will be a square space formed by the bottom edges of the 2 triangle strips. Using D, pick up 15 sts on the edge of the first of these 2 strips; then pick up

15 sts along the other edge, for a total of 30 sts. Knit 1 foundation row. Now work a garter stitch miter on these 30 sts as follows:

ROW 1 (RS): K13, [K2tog] twice, K13

ROW 2 AND EVERY WS ROW: Knit every st

ROW 3: K12, K2tog twice, K12

ROW 5: K11, [K2tog] twice, K11

Continue decreasing 2 sts at the center of every RS row until 2 sts remain.

Last Row: (This will be a WS row.) Slip 1, K1, psso, fasten off the last stitch.

Using the chart to determine the direction of the strips, make 5 more blocks. Join the 6 blocks as shown. Make 5 more triangle strips. Attach as shown, and make the last 6 corner squares. Using E, make a border as described on p. 75.

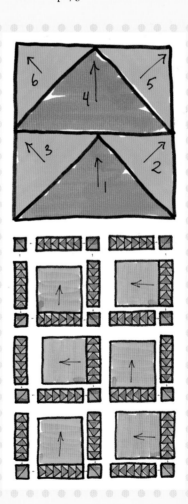

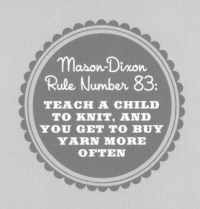

Chapter Four

FAMBLY*PROJECKS

I WAS DYING TO TEACH DAVID TO KNIT. It was one of the ten PARENTAL COMMANDMENTS: Thou shalt teach thy kid TO*KNIT.

Grown-ups are allowed to
use kids' spool-knitting
supplies for making
I-cord. But grown-ups
must return all kid tools
before kids discover their
world has been invaded.

THE FINE ART OF GETTING KIDS TO KNIT

★ ★ ★ ★ ★ ★ ★ ★ ★

ANN · Robin Smith is a second-grade teacher at Ensworth School in Nashville. She has taught hundreds of children to knit. I have been inspired and amazed by the way she has created a culture of wee fiber artists. She makes it look very easy.

Q: The first time I saw your classroom full of kids knitting at 7:30 in the morning, I was stunned—boys, girls, all arriving early at school so they can hang out with you. What are the challenges of teaching children to knit?

Ann ✳ Several days a week I drive hookup. *Hookup* is Nashvillese for *carpool*. The art of hookup at David's school is a little like a Masonic rite: mysterious, governed by unwritten rules, and when you get right down to it, a little pointless to anyone watching from the outside.

You have your latecomers who breeze in at 3:15 and avoid the winding line of mom bombs. Then you have your early birds, the moms who arrive at 2:30 to be the first to scoop up their young children. Is it necessary to arrive at school a half-hour early? Not really. But it's where you'll find me several times a week, because it gives me guaranteed, high-quality knitting time.

On a nice day I'll sit on the bench by the front door, and I'll trade juicy tidbits with moms who are going in and out. At three o'clock, the youngest kids start to appear, and that's when the little boys and girls swarm around me to study my knitting. They stare with the blank curiosity of a creature from the Galapagos. Three or four will gather, and one always says, "What are you making?" When I show them a Fair Isle sweater worked in the round, one girl asks, "When do you start picking up stitches for the sleeves?" "How do you keep the colors from tangling?" "What size needles are those?" "That yarn sure is thin." For second graders, they show an unusual interest in knitting, because, the fact is, they know a lot about knitting.

At David's school, there are teachers who understand that knitting is a great thing for young fingers: it teaches small-motor coordination, math, and especially, it teaches children to be calm, to sit and work at something in a quiet way. It proved to be a big part of my young fella's life.

David and the Eight Pound Ball of Yarn

Once a child knows how to knit, it's not long before she starts helping her friend. We love that.

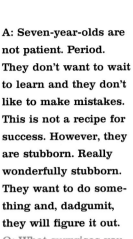

A: Seven-year-olds are not patient. Period. They don't want to wait to learn and they don't like to make mistakes. This is not a recipe for success. However, they are stubborn. Really wonderfully stubborn. They want to do something and, dadgumit, they will figure it out.

Q: What surprises you about your students and their knitting?

A: I am constantly surprised by how much they are comforted by their knitting. Also, they love to knit for other people, and that is quite heartwarming. Boys are so good at knitting—once I get their dads to stop worrying about the long-term consequences . . .

David's evolution into Fiber Arts Boy began in first grade, when he came home with a utensil that looked like a slingshot missing the sling. It was a lucet, a wooden tool they were told medieval people used to make cords. David took to lucetting the way Rumpelstiltskin took to spinning straw into gold, and after a few days, he had a pile of lucet cord.

So did his friends. They also learned finger knitting, which is basically lucetting without a lucet. Being a pack rat, David started a ball of cord, and before long, he began accepting lucet cord and finger knitting from his friends. The ball grew and grew. He took it to school every day, where they would unwind it on the playground to see how far it would go, then wind it back up. After a week it was so big that he couldn't carry it. When we weighed it, the ball was more than eight pounds.

At home, the eight-pound ball of yarn became a bit of a burden. It wouldn't fit in a cabinet or on a shelf, so it sat out on the floor in our den. One day, when I was using it for a footstool, I noticed how it looked very much like a ball of yarn, only supersized. Well, you know how irresistible a ball of yarn is, so I made a quick trip to buy some big needles. Of course, David did not let his ball go without a lot of haggling. A regular camel trader he was, going on about how much the ball meant to him, how much work he and his friends had put into it. Ach! Enough with the sales pitch! I paid him twenty bucks.

I had never knitted with such huge needles. It was more like construction work than knitting. It took a while to get much speed, but I was hooked. This stuff had a nice spongy feel, and it clearly wanted to be a rug.

The ball of yarn went with us on vacation to Pawleys Island, South Carolina, where it had a great time. I taught two kids to knit. One was a six-year-old girl who said not a single word until she had finished an entire row of clown wig–colored bouclé. She looked up, blinked, and said, "I get it." The other was my four-year-old nephew, Will. Every time we finished a stitch, he would nod, smile knowingly, and say in his earnest way, "Off. Pops. Jaaaaack." Hubbo's sister Liz rediscovered the lost knitter lurking in her soul, and muttered "This could get addicting" as she spread the heavy rug over her knees. It was communal knitting at its most pointless. After a week we had knitted about four pounds of yarn.

At that point the rug had a promising, folk-arty look at one end, and a World Tour of Acrylic at the other. We headed into a big stretch of white, which I feared would make or break the subtle color rhythms. Or something. It turned out not to matter. The rug looks totally kooky, seven feet of this 'n' that, but I love it anyway. The eight-pound ball of yarn was my first experience in looking around, at my very feet, for a project. Sometimes it takes a seven-year-old's obsession to open your eyes.

Places We Have Tried to Knit and Failed

🔪 FUNERAL

Well, I didn't actually try to knit, but throughout the service I kept thinking about the handbag under my chair and the little scarf I was cooking up in the most colorful Diakeito. As I sat in the far back, one of a jillion folks paying their respects, I had the passing thought: *He would have wanted me to knit during his eulogy. He would have liked that.*

🛍 WAL-MART

No matter how long the line is, there is not enough time to get that mitten out of the Ziploc bag.

🚧 INTERSTATE

Even the stretch of I-24 between Murfreesboro and Winchester is not straight enough to allow for driving with the knees. Please. Do not try this. If you're in charge of a moving vehicle, you're going to have trouble maintaining your gauge.

🏛 NON-PROFIT BOARD MEETING

Again, a big crowd, me in the back. What do they care? Those suits think I'm a housewife? I'll show them what a housewife does during a board meeting. Damn straight I'm knitting— I've got two hot water bottle covers to finish before Christmas.

⛪ CENTERING PRAYER

WWJD? He'd knit. Sure he would. Don't nuns knit a lot? Or something? I kept wondering, *Do people think this is offensive?*

🏟 YANKEE STADIUM

Game 7 of the Boston-New York 2003 American League Championship Series. I had managed to get my knitting through the bag security inspection. With all the Boston fans in the stands, I didn't want to do anything that might turn the crowd ugly. I could just see the *New York Post* headline: "IMPALED!!!!!!!!!"

Potholder loops are available at any craft or discount store. The nylon ones are kind of a bummer: they can be used only on pots that are less than 350 degrees hot. What kind of lame-o potholder is that? Once again, natural fibers win the day.

POTHOLDER MANIA

This rug got me to thinking about knitted rugs. Could I create a rug that would have the same sponginess (as comfy as my ugly bedroom slippers!) but in colors that did not include clown-wig bouclé yarn? You know—a rug that might actually be attractive?

Those big needles were a revelation to me: I could get an inch of knitting done in a few minutes. Until I tried those tube-sized whoppers, I had been intrigued by small needles. It was satisfying to create the thin fabrics that suited our Nashville climate—the few heavy sweaters I had made were useful only when freakishly cold weather came through.

But a rug. Any floor can use a rug. Floors don't care how itchy and chunky their rugs are. In my rug research, I discovered something called a spiral rug, a simple coiled garter-stitch strip that was pure elegance. Leave it to the Shakers—when you're living that childless lifestyle, you can put a lot of energy into floor coverings. The spiral rug was totally modern looking, like the Yellow Brick Road except, um, no Munchkins. *Someday,* I thought, *that rug will be mine.*

We left for a week in the mountains of Grundy County, Tennessee, to a place called the Monteagle Assembly. The Assembly was created in 1882 as a summer church camp and chautauqua. It is a collection of Victorian cottages which are laid out in the woods like a small town. It's the sort of place that makes you want to do quaint things. Somewhere in the Assembly's elaborate bylaws is the regulation: "The Assembly shall promote the creation of potholders using small loops made from leftover socks."

When my friend Frannie told me that there were potholder looms to be had, it took four false starts to find the house where the arts and crafts classes were held. Shady Delle feels like the arts and crafts building at the camp you really loved: rough wood floors, open windows, and a trove of craft supplies. We found a box full of potholder looms and a cup where you left your $5. David was amazed that people left money, perfectly good money, without anybody stealing it. "The Assembly is another world," I told him, staring dreamily at the row of watercolors drying on the wall. I looked down at David, who had edged up to the cup of honorable bucks. "Hey—put that back!"

David made potholders the way those Peruvian women knit sweaters: really fast and really well. It took two hours to exhaust our supply of loops. My friend Cary, being a veteran of the Assembly, understood the extreme craft requirements of the Assembly and had brought a vast bowl of potholder loops. As the moms sat on Cary's porch enjoying the late afternoon and that flat, empty feeling a hot day with children gives you, David and George and Jack and Zara and Douglas furiously cranked out potholders.

The ones I coveted were made of cotton loops: heavy, almost stiff squares of tightly woven loops. What a fantastic rug these squares would make. I ordered a freight train's worth of loops, so that my little pieceworker would crank out squares that I would then somehow knit together. Poifect.

The law of unintended consequences is no more apparent than in a house with small boys. When my precious stash of Harrisville Friendly Potholder Loops arrived, David burrowed into them like a badger in the dirt. But something weird happened. He wasn't making potholders as I'd planned. He was knotting the loops together to make a long, long chain of loops. I'd never seen such a linear boy. But as I watched him, I realized that he might have found a way to create a superspongy yarn that would give me the cushy rug of my dreams.

Floors don't care how itchy and *chunky* their rugs are.

SURELY SOMETHING WILL COME OF THIS

A new four-pound ball of yarn was born: hundreds of potholder loops chained together. David was balky there toward the end. He started hinting about workplace conditions. ("Mommmm, we don't have any *good* snacks except Pop-Tarts, and I don't like strawberry.") At any moment I thought Sally Field was going to show up in our kitchen, climb up on the table, and hold up a sign that read "UNION." Let's just say that a last-minute marathon bargaining session took place in a smoky back room, and crisis was averted.

We had used all ten shades of Harrisville Friendly Loops, and our ball was a springy, bouncy, *Free to Be . . . You and Me* rainbow of love. I commenced knitting. So chunky. It was the chunkiest thing I'd ever knitted. I had found it: a yarn too thick to knit. I punted on my plan for a spiral rug—this stuff was just too much—and ended up with a garter-stitch mat that will outlive the pyramids.

I moved on. I had a final weapon in my arsenal: the rag ball.

Twice a year in Nashville, there is a gargantuan antiques show/junkfest called the Tailgate Antiques Show. Arcana abounds there, from moose heads to jewelry made from hair. The fiber arts are always well represented, with at least one nonfunctioning yarn swift for sale. One day I noticed a wooden box filled with rag balls—inch-wide strips of vintage calico and ticking wound into dense balls. They were so beautiful that they had to come home with me, but as I drove down Briley Parkway I noticed something: My car had suddenly begun to smell like the basement of my grandmother's house. A little musty. Dank. Whiffy. The rag balls were telling me the story of their lives, and what a tale it was.

No matter. I knew that these little whiffers were going to meet their destiny in the rug of my dreams.

The pattern for a spiral rug is lovely in its simplicity: It begins with two stitches, then increases into a long, long strip that goes until you want to barf from tedium. I persevered, remembering that some of my proudest knitting achievements came when I knitted through my fears. I wanted that spiral rug. Somehow, I was going to finish.

WILL IT KNIT?
✔ **CREPE PAPER STREAMERS**
Yes if you're careful.
✔ **CAUTION TAPE**
Yes.
✗ **MASKING TAPE**
No and it was stupid to try.

We like the treasure hunt of finding vintage rag balls at flea markets and online—we will someday find a long-lost diamond ring in the center of one. But making your own rag balls is a fine use of old clothes, and provides a Little Red Hen moment of true start-to-finish craftiness.

THE HORSE DECIDES TO DRINK

I was dying to teach David to knit. It was one of the Ten Parental Commandments: Thou shalt teach thy kid to knit. As I sat on my bench at school, I'd see those sturdy little boys chugging through their hats, and I wanted David to be one of them. But I knew better than to push it, after many failed episodes of excessive mommy encouragement. (See "Let's Go Bowling!" "A Trip to the Theater!" and "Swimming Is Going to Be So Great!") I figured that his teachers at school would get him started, so I resisted the mighty urge to give him some stumpy needles and big yarn.

Then, one day, the way a long-awaited cheetah creeps out of the tall grass, David sat down beside me as I worked on the rug. "I want to knit," he announced.

"Sure. OK. Hold on," I said, sidling out of the room so as not to spook my quarry. Out of sight, moving fast, I dug up some yarn and needles, and verrrry casually came back into the sunroom.

He watched me make three stitches, said, "OK, I get it," and started to knit, exactly the way he learned to ride a bike: just like that. No dropped stitches, no mystery weirdo parts. He cranked out the row then said, "Now what?"

I think a lot about what's easy and what's hard. Things that come easily aren't worth much, I've always thought. But here was my fella, knitting like a professional on his first try, and it occurred to me: Why am I worrying so much? If he wants to do something, he decides to do it. I can only give him the rollerblades or, in this case, the tasteful English yarn.

"Well," I said. "We can do a rug if you want." With that, I passed him the long strip of knitting for the spiral rug, and my most linear of boys set to work.

SUPERFANCY POTHOLDER LOOP RUG

This rug is the kind of back-door mat that will withstand a Category 4 hurricane. It is the stoutest thing ever knitted. When a meteor hits Earth, this rug will remain as the lone clue to a lost civilization.

MATERIALS: Harrisville Looms potholder loops. If you want to get all particular, here's a recipe for how many bags you'll need for your rug:

1 loop = 6" (15 cm)
approx 37 loops/package
So, you can expect around 19' (5.8m) of loops per bag.
20 bags = approx 380' (115.8m) of super-spongy supernatural loopy yarn. This results in a rug approximately 22" x 28" (56 cm x 71 cm). Add more bags if you're craving something larger.
Size 35 (19mm) needles

GAUGE: Whatever you get is the right gauge! You can't lose!
Get a small fry. Have him or her open all the bags. Have the fry chain-loop the loops to make a giant ball of the chunkiest yarn you'll ever see. CO 26 sts. Knit in garter stitch until you practically run out, then BO. You win extra points if you finish with exactly one potholder loop remaining to be woven in.

The Dizzy Rug is cosmic. Imagine it with changing blocks of color. Imagine it in a stout wool. Imagine knitting forty feet of it and making the Longest Thing Ever Knitted.

DIZZY RUG

This rug uses rag balls—either flea market finds or ones you've made from your own scraps. If you'd rather use yarn, this would look great in a super-chunky wool or thick cotton. Sewing up the rug in a contrasting color is key to making the spiral blast off.

SIZE: Approx 30" (76 cm) diameter

MATERIALS: Three-pound (27.5g) ball of 1" (2.5 cm)-wide fabric strips
Size 15 (10 mm) needles

GAUGE: Do not sweat it. It will look great. This is a long strip of garter stitch, beginning very narrow, widening to 8 stitches, then decreasing on the final outside lap back to one stitch.

CO 2 sts.

ROW 1: K2.

ROW 2: Sl 1, k1.

ROWS 3-12: Repeat Rows 1 and 2.

ROW 13: K1, CO 1 using backward loop method, k1.

ROW 14: Sl 1, k2.

ROW 15: K3.

ROW 16: Sl 1, k2.

ROW 17: K3.

ROW 18: Sl 1, k2.

ROW 19: K1, CO 1, k2.

ROW 20: Sl 1, k3.

ROW 21: K4.

ROWS 22-26: Repeat Rows 20 and 21.

ROW 27: K1, CO 1, k3.

ROW 28: Sl 1, k4.

ROW 29: K5.

ROWS 30-40: Repeat Rows 28 and 29.

ROW 41: K1, CO 1, k4.

ROW 42: Sl 1, k5.

ROW 43: K6.

ROWS 44-58: Repeat Rows 42 and 43.

ROW 59: K1, CO 1, k5.

ROW 60: Sl 1, k6.

ROW 61: K7.

ROWS 62-82: Repeat Rows 60 and 61.

ROW 83: K1, CO 1, k6.

ROW 84: Sl 1, k7.

ROW 85: K8.

Repeat Rows 84 and 85 until rug is one lap shy of the size you want.

In the final lap, decrease seven stitches evenly around the rug. To decrease, k2tog in the center of a row. When you get to one stitch, you're done.

Finishing

Large table required. Using a contrasting rag or fabric shade (as long a piece as you can manage) and a big tapestry needle, start at center and carefully noodge the beginning of the spiral into place. Be careful to sew the strip so the rug lays flat—the rows of garter stitch should radiate out straight from the center. If they slant, you get the Dreaded Cupping Effect.

DISHRAG RUG

A great kid project: Use the Ballband Dishcloth pattern from Chapter 1, but with a heavier yarn and 12" (30.5 cm) squares. Get your kid slipping those stitches, make six squares, and sew them together. Adorable! The color possibilities are endless.

A child with enough yarn can crank a dishcloth rug in remarkably little time. But plan to help with the sew-up: there's no sense in revealing too soon the grim truth of rug manufacturing.

These Circles of Fun
turn into polka dots
when strewn across a
room. You can make
several, and your child
will pretend they are
lily pads for frogleap-
ing. Or planets. A
caveat: Unless indoor
skating is your favorite
activity, we encourage
a rug pad under all
knitted rugs.

CIRCLE-OF-FUN RUG

In the midst of an endless journey into rugs, this pinwheely rug gave me a sense of accomplishment when all other efforts were not panning out. It's a great rug for a parent-child effort. Parent makes the pinwheel center, marveling at his or her cleverness at shortrowing. Child cranks out outer strips until new episode of *Scooby Doo* comes on. Parent finishes rug, feels warmhearted at parent-child effort, which child no longer remembers.

SIZE: 38" (96 cm) diameter

MATERIALS: Wool Pak Yarns NZ 14 Ply by Baabajoes Wool Company, [9 oz (250 g) hanks, each approx 310yds (284 m), wool] 2 hanks each in 7 berry (A) and 6 red (B), and 1 hank each in 48 persimmon (C) and 41 apple blossom (D)

Size 10½ (7 mm) needles or size needed to achieve gauge

GAUGE: 13 sts + 24 rows = 4" (10 cm) over garter st.

Note: All yarns are held double in this pattern.

Holding A and B together, CO 32 sts.

ROW 1: K2. Do not knit the other 30 stitches. Turn work so that the 2 stitches just knitted are now on the left needle and the other 30 stitches are on the right needle. Move working yarn to back of work.

ROW 2: Sl 1 (purlwise for all sl st), k1.

ROW 3: K4.

ROW 4: Sl 1, k3.

ROW 5: K6.

ROW 6: Sl 1, k5.

ROW 7: K8.

ROW 8: Sl 1, k7.

ROW 9: K10.

ROW 10: Sl 1, k9.

Avoidance of the End: As you make the pinwheel, carry the yarn not in use along the outside edge of the pinwheel. It makes a decorative little border, but mostly, it saves you a lot of work.

ROW 11: K12.

ROW 12: Sl 1, k11.

ROW 13: K14.

ROW 14: Sl 1, k13.

ROW 15: K16.

ROW 16: Sl 1, k15.

Are you noticing a pattern here? Keep at this until you have completed the pie wedge. Your wedge will have 32 rows at the outside edge. Do not cut yarns A & B. Join C & D. To minimize ends to be sewn in, carry A & B along the outside edge of the pie wedge. Simply lift A & B over C & D before you begin a row at the outside edge. Repeat Rows 1-32 as above. Continue in this way, carrying yarn not in use along outside edge of pie wedges, until you have a whole pie of 12 wedges in alternating colors. On the final pie wedge, BO on Row 31. Cut the yarn, leaving five feet (1.5 m) of yarn, and with tapestry needle thread through all center loops and pull tight. Sew edges of pie wedges together. Result: one pinwheelish pie.

Next, the circle of fun begins. Holding B & C together, CO 10 stitches. Knit in garter stitch for approximately three years, or until strip fits outside of pinwheelish pie. BO.

Next, holding A & B together, CO 20 stitches, knit for approximately seven-and-a-half years, or until strip fits outside of the first strip. BO.

Finishing

Sew strips around the pie. Be sure to have a large table at your disposal, so that you can lay the rug out as you sew it up. You want to ease the strips around the pie without the Dreaded Cupping Effect (strip stretched too tightly) or, worse, the Wavy Warbles (strip not stretched enough).

Kay

POSTSCRIPT: CALAMARI KNITTING

Inspired by knitting with potholder loops slip-knotted together, we thought, as we always seem to do: Can't we knit this with something else? Must we keep attracting attention to ourselves by buying so many potholder loops?

Here is one of those rare and precious things: a project that kids find really and truly fun, that does not make a mess, destroy your house or your eardrums, or otherwise drive you crazy. It's so much fun that you have to force yourself to let the kids do it and not hog it all for yourself. It's Calamari Knitting. Don't look it up; the term doesn't exist. I made it up.

I saw a project in *Marie-Claire Idées*, a French magazine for the chic and crafts-obsessed French woman. It was a sling seat for a folding lawn chair. It was crocheted from strips that were cut from plastic shopping bags. *Oh, la-la*, I thought, *C'est tres funky, n'est-ce pas?*

The perennial problem of knitting with strips of anything is this: How do you attach the strips together into a single, continuous, knittable material, without this task becoming your Life's Work? In the case of the French Lawn Chair, *Marie-Claire Idées* had an ingenious, elegant solution. When you get right down to it, bags are simply cylinders with handles at the top, and a bottom at the bottom. The clever Frenchies at *Marie-Claire* simply cut off the handles and the bottom, and then cut the cylinder, crosswise, into narrow strips that look for all the world like rings of calamari. Then—and here's the part the kids love—you slipknot these rings together. *Just like potholder loops.* And when you knit your calamari-ring yarn, the smooth slipknots disappear into the fabric of the knitting.

Folding my fifth load of laundry one day, I had a Lucid Moment. I looked at a T-shirt. Like a grocery bag, it was a cylinder; a cylinder with a neck, shoulders, and sleeves. If you cut across the shirt in a line from armpit to armpit, and cut the resulting cylinder, cross-wise, into narrow strips, *you could do Calamari Knitting with old T-shirts.*

RIGHT: A rug is the true, best use of calamari yarn. There is no garment that calls for yarn which knits at this sort of gauge. Except, maybe, Biohazard Level IV protective gear.
OPPSITE PAGE: Calamari knitting = knitting as craft project. Please know that at some point, children will want to see how far their calamari yarn will go. (The answer: at least two times around your house.)

Think of all the soft, cylindrical stuff you can cut up and turn into something knittable! A skirt, dress, or pullover shirt—any garment without buttons. Cotton print fabrics make really nice knittable rags. Pant legs. *Jeans* legs. The softer the fabric, the less bumpy the slipknots will be. Sleeves. Any old pullover sweater, provided it won't unravel when you cut it. If it's wool, try felting it first. You are limited only by the number of cylindrical garments you can commandeer.

It's so much *fun* that you have to force yourself to

let the kids do it and not hog it all for yourself.

Mason-Dixon
Rule Number 368:
**DON'T TAKE
ANY CRAP
ABOUT BEING
A KNITTER.**

Chapter Five
OVER THE TOP, OR, TRUE *ARTISTES

· ·

Some of these knitters ARE FAMOUS IN THE WORLD OF FIBER ARTS... OTHERS ARE UNKNOWN, but share * the same GIVE-'EM-HELL SPIRIT of just picking up the needles AND MAKING STUFF.

· ·

Kay ✳ Knitting is an endless puzzle with innumerable surprises. Over the years, I've spent countless hours hunched over in my chair, staring at the pattern, then at the needles in my hands, then at the pattern again. By doing this, I keep discovering new marvels. When I was a new knitter, it could be as elementary as the discovery that when you are ribbing, after you have done a row or two, the stitches actually tell you when you should knit and when you should purl. If this seems very obvious to you, dear reader, try to remember when you first discovered it. Not the first time somebody told you, but the first time you really saw it in your hands.

Another epiphany occurred when I mechanically followed the directions for knitting a pocket lining and "placing" a pocket. You bind off a series of stitches just as wide as the pocket lining, right in the middle of a row. Then, on the next row, when you get to the bound-off stitches, you put the live stitches of the pocket lining onto your needle and knit across them. I performed this little maneuver on faith. I couldn't "see" it in my head until I had done it. Will ya lookie here—I'll be damned if it's not a pocket.

I hope to go on like this for the rest of my life: knitting and discovering new insights and tricks along the way. Learning, from doing, how to "read" my knitting, and how to visualize the construction of garments. But somewhere along the way, I started to notice that some knitters were approaching it much differently. Instead of following patterns, and increasing their store of knowledge by bits and pieces, they were doing what for me was unthinkable: they were picking up needles and yarn and making things they saw in their heads. They were winging it, people! Some of these knitters are famous in the world of fiber arts, as writers, designers, and true artists. Others are unknown, but share the same give-'em-hell spirit of just picking up the needles and making stuff.

At first, this approach struck me as delusions of grandeur. Why, in a world in which so many designers are creating amazing garments, would I want to attempt it on my own? No matter how hard I tried, I could not possibly make anything that would be half as good.

Kaycam

A pile of scrappy, stripey squares inspired by a knitted throw pictured in Kaffe Fassett's *Passionate Patchwork*. The Kaffe, he is not afraid to mix up the fiber arts. Super Fantastic!

There are very good reasons to try. For one thing, despite the many patterns out there, there may not exist the one perfect thing that you want. I found this to be true of blankets. Whenever a book came out with knitted blankets in it, even baby blankets, I pored over it. I wanted to make blankets as keepsakes that would be kept for generations. But I saw few knitted blanket patterns that captured the feeling I had in mind: non-fussy, timeless, elemental, perhaps a little Amish. There was a lot of lace and intarsia out there, and blankets that looked like overgrown sweaters, but I couldn't find *my* blanket.

I had a breakthrough one day, and it was thanks to my incorrigible eBay habit. I had bought a used copy of Kaffe Fassett's book *Passionate Patchwork*. I bought it even though I was not all that passionate about patchwork. I don't even sew, thanks to an ugly encounter with an elastic waistband in seventh-grade Home Economics class. But I had run through all Kaffe's knitting books, so when I came across his non-knitting titles I bought them out of curiosity. There, on page 12 of *Passionate Patchwork*, was a knitted blanket hanging from the window of a painted green caravan. It was a patchwork of knitted squares. The squares were striped randomly in contrasting cotton yarn, and arranged with the stripes going in alternate directions, for a basketweave effect. Now that, I thought, is what I'm talking about.

It hit me, suddenly, that I could have had this idea. That I could make a blanket like this, using my own choices of color and my own striping patterns. That this would be satisfying to do.

So I made twelve patches, which still sit in a box in my stash. Because soon after that, I discovered log cabin knitting, which knocked me on my keister. I'm not sure, though, that I would have been ready for log cabin knitting, if I hadn't seen that striped blanket hanging on the green caravan.

ONLY IN NEW YORK

KAY • There I was, trudging up Park Avenue in a freezing wind. Ahead of me, also trudging, a woman wearing a phantasmagoric, multicolor, full-length crocheted coat.

Well, of course I spoke to her—we had a blog to put out, right?

I said, "That's a gorgeous coat...Did you make it?"

With quiet pride, she said, "Yes."

I asked, "Did you design it?" (I thought there was a good chance that she had because the coat was so original.)

Again, a modest "Yes."

Me: "May I take your picture?" Mind you, it was freezing. It was dark. She looked like she had someplace to go.

(Graciously) "Yes."

So I took a very blurry photo of a forbearing artisan.

And then came the only-in-New-York part. She handed me a postcard giving the details of the exhibition of her work in a gallery uptown.

It turns out that this gracious paragon of patience was none other than Xenobia Bailey, the artist who works wonders of color and sculpture in crochet, whom I had read about in magazines. The Xenobia Bailey who imagined, and then actually made, the amazing seven-foot-tall "Sistah Paradise's Great Wall of Fire Revival Tent." That Xenobia Bailey.

I wish I had been able to take a better picture.

COULD IT BE THAT IT WAS ALL SO SIMPLE THEN?

A h, the mitered square. Miters are one of the most addictive of knitting pleasures. I came late to miters. I had briefly looked at the wonderful books by Horst Schulz and Vivian Høxbro, which give lots of ideas for things that you can make by knitting miters onto each other in different configurations. This blanket began with a trip to Sarah Bradberry's wonderful Web site, www.knitting-and.com.

This Australia-based author of knitting books and patterns offers a collection of free patterns for all manner of afghans and other items. One of them, the Psychedelic Squares Afghan, was my starting point. I devised my color scheme, a plan for the number and arrangement of squares, how they would be joined, and how the blanket would be bordered. It took me forever, but I was happy the whole way through. Someday scientists will confirm my belief that knitting a miter floods the brain with endorphins, which explains why they are so addictive.

The most fun part, though, was playing with colors. For this, I drew on my many years of meditating on the brilliant color work of Kaffe Fassett. Under Kaffe's spell, I have come to love unusual color juxtapositions, layering several shades of the same colors to add depth and a sense of movement, and irregularities that add liveliness to repeating patterns. If you find my choices hilarious, hideous, or just plain horrible, please don't blame Kaffe Fassett. He gave me the courage to trust my own eyes, but he's not responsible for the results.

Don't be shy about
letting company see
that you've knitted an
entire bedspread.
(They already know
you're crazy.)

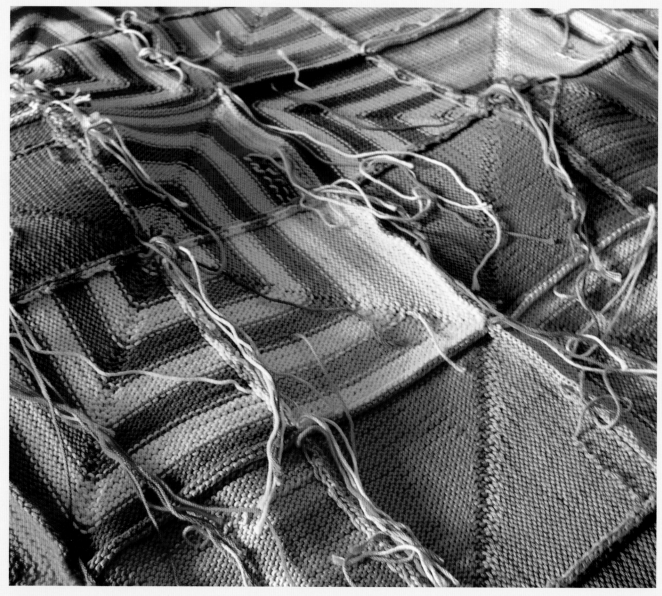

The seam side of a stripey mitered square blanket is not for the faint of heart. Sewing in these ends is The Right Thing to Do, but lightning will *probably* not strike you if you tie them in sturdy square knots and trim neatly.

MITERED SQUARE BLANKET

SIZE: 70" x 56" (178 cm x 142 cm)

MATERIALS: Cotton Classic by Tahki Yarns/Tahki·Stacy Charles, Inc., [1¾ oz (50 g), 108 yds (100 m), mercerized cotton] 40 hanks in assorted colors
Size 6 (4 mm) needles or size needed to achieve gauge

GAUGE: 20 sts + 28 rows = 4" (10 cm) over St st.

Striped Miter (make 80)

Each miter uses 2 colors, A and B.
Using A, CO 72 sts.

ROW 1: K33, ssk, [k2tog] twice, k to end.

ROW 2 AND ALL EVEN NUMBERED ROWS: Purl.

ROW 3: K32, [ssk] twice, k2tog, k to end.

ROW 5: K30, ssk, [k2tog] twice, k to end.

ROW 7: Using B, K29, [ssk] twice, k2tog, k to end.

ROW 9: K27, ssk, [k2tog] twice, k to end.

ROW 11: K26, [ssk] twice, k2tog, k to end.

ROW 13: Using A, K24, ssk, [k2tog] twice, k to end.

ROW 15: K23, [ssk] twice, k2tog, k to end.

ROW 17: K21, ssk, [k2tog] twice, k to end.

ROW 19: Using B, K20, [ssk] twice, k2tog, k to end.

ROW 21: K18, ssk, [k2tog] twice, k to end.

ROW 23: K17, [ssk] twice, k2tog, k to end.

ROW 25: Using A, K15, ssk, [k2tog] twice, k to end.

ROW 27: K14, [ssk] twice, k2tog, k to end.

ROW 29: K12, ssk, [k2tog] twice, k to end.

ROW 31: Using B, K11, [ssk] twice, k2tog, k to end.

ROW 33: K9, ssk, [k2tog] twice, k to end.

ROW 35: K8, [ssk] twice, k2tog, k to end.

ROW 37: Using A, K6, ssk, [k2tog] twice, k to end.

ROW 39: K5, [ssk] twice, k2tog, k to end.

ROW 41: K3, ssk, [k2tog] twice, k to end.

ROW 43: Using B, K2, [ssk] twice, k2tog, k to end.

ROW 45: Ssk, [k2tog] twice.

ROW 47: Sl 1, k2tog, psso.

Fasten off remaining stitch.

Block the miters by dampening them, and straightening the edges. Allow to dry.

Using mattress stitch, seam the miters into 20 blocks of 4, then seam the blocks into 4 vertical strips of 5 blocks. Then seam the strips together.

Sew in all ends.

Border

Make a mitered garter stitch border using the "picture frame" technique described on page 75. Each edge has 4 stripes composed of 2 garter ridges per stripe.

Lightly press the blanket. Treat it like the heirloom it is. Put it someplace where every visitor to your home will see it.

TECHNICAL HINTS

How to Calculate Yarn Quantities for a Smaller or Larger Blanket

A 1 3/4 oz (50 g) skein [108 yds (100 m)] will yield between 2 and 3 miters, so once you have decided how many 4-miter blocks your blanket will have, you can estimate the quantity of yarn you need to buy. Or you can do as I did. I started out with 20 skeins in various colors, and as I knitted my way through the miters, I bought more skeins in colors that appealed to me as my preferences emerged. I'm glad I didn't choose all the colors at the beginning, because some of my initial color combinations were not as pleasing to me as the ones I happened upon later.

Tips on Stripes ★ Do not cut the yarn between stripes; carry the color not in use up the side. When changing colors for the first row of a stripe, pull the new color around your needle from behind the old color. Immediately before starting the third and fifth rows of a stripe, cross the old color over the working yarn before knitting the first stitch. This will prevent a loop of the old yarn from forming at the right edge.

If You Hate to Sew in Ends ★ If you despair of sewing in all those ends, tie two ends together at a time into snug square knots, trim them to 2" (5 cm), and let them dangle on the wrong side.

NOVELTY YARN
WE'RE WORKING ON
★ ★ ★ ★ ★ ★ ★ ★ ★ ★ ★ ★

We have decided to go into the yarn business. Watch for our forthcoming announcement about these exciting new products:

☞ JELLEAUX: A nylon ladder yarn with globules of fruit-flavored gelatin. Gemlike colors.

☞ LESTER: Recycled strands of old mops reclaimed from school cafeterias in east Tennessee.

☞ ZOLOFTY: Tangles a lot, but it doesn't really bother you anymore.

☞ NAVIGATOR: Sport utility weight. 1 stitch = 1 foot.

☞ POUND OF WOE: 50% burlap/50% fiberglass.

COLOR "RULES"

When I started knitting miters for this blanket, I made some rules about how I would use the colors. Why? We don't need no stinkin' rules, do we?

Well, actually, I do. Rules make it so much easier to make decisions. If I had to make a new color decision for each of eighty miters, it would start to seem like work. Having a rule keeps it fun, especially since I feel free to violate my rule when inspiration (or accident) strikes, and I get that naughty thrill of flouting authority.

So I came up with my own rule. I had chosen very vivid, juicy colors, such as orange, purple, and citrus greens. I had also chosen neutral, blah colors like gray, khaki, and drab green. I liked the way putting a juicy color next to a blah color did two things: It toned down the brightness of the juicy (two juicies together could, in some cases, cause retina damage), but gave a new vibrancy to the blah.

At the yarn store, I noticed that whenever I threw pale pastels (baby blue, petal pink), primary colors (fire engine red, royal blue), black or white into the mix of juicies and blahs, the pastels looked washed-out, and the primaries were depressingly flat. White had a deadening effect on adjacent colors, and black drew the eye away from the sea of color. So, except for a couple of early miters that I made before I figured this out, I avoided pastels, primaries, black and white.

Sometimes, mid-miter, I would hit a knot in the yarn, or the ball would run out. In either case, instead of continuing in the same color, I saw an opportunity to change colors in an unexpected spot. I would choose a new juicy or blah color, as appropriate, and continue knitting. This adds that touch of random irregularity that our eyes love because it provides relief from the rigor of the pattern.

Kaycam

JUICIES AND BLAHS
In striped miters, as in log cabin, you start by playing with colors. Romp through your stash! This is the first selection of "juicies and blahs" for the Mitered Square Blanket. Many trips to the yarn store were yet to come.

SOME (SIGNIFICANT) ASSEMBLY REQUIRED

When you're done knitting and it's time to put your eighty-square blanket together, I highly recommend that you not skip this step: Sit down and cry. Aw, just kidding. Usually, sewing up is my least favorite part of knitting. In this case, as I knit my way through the eighty squares, I became more and more eager to see how this profusion of colors would look together. The heroic scale of the project (I was knitting a queen-size *bedspread*, something that for all I knew, no woman had done since the late eighteenth century) made me actually look forward to sewing up. I was a woman possessed.

The *raison d'être*, the *je ne sais quoi*, the *sine qua non* of the mitered square, is that the stripes all meet each other with precision. Neatness counts.

How do we enhance the neatness of our sew-up? We block, people!

Unlike Ann, I rarely pin things down when I'm blocking. I never use gingham or striped sheets or a fancy-ass board with measurements printed on it. I just wet pieces, flatten them out, straighten their edges, and blast them with a shot or two of steam from my mighty Rowenta. Then I leave them to dry, slowly in the case of cotton. When they are dry, the edges are perfectly flat and much easier to sew together.

When you're done with all that seaming, which will have taken you several sessions of Kung Fu concentration, it's time to put a border on your blanket. A borderless blanket looks naked and its seams are less sturdy. Besides, the border is another opportunity for color play. You can highlight one of the colors in the blanket (so that it actually goes with something else you own, perhaps), or introduce something new. A black border is ultra classy. A white border says "summer." A thin border says, "I'm tired of knitting this damn blanket."

Kaycam

NEATNESS COUNTS
Use mattress stitch, and don't hesitate to re-do a section of seaming when the stitches don't line up exactly at the intersections. You made too many squares to have bumps at the corners.

ODE TO ROWENTA

KAY · *Is it possible to love a steam iron?*

If you block a lot of handknits, the answer is, "Heckyeah!" My beloved Rowenta is right up there with my engagement ring and photo albums on the list of things I'd try to grab and take with me if the house were burning down.

I was raised in Nebraska, where self-sufficiency is prized. Children earn their keep from an early age. Busting sod, de-tasseling corn, feeding chickens, that sort of thing. Even so, my parents took it a little far. My Mom the Insane Clean Freak made me "responsible" for doing all the family's ironing.

This was practically child abuse, because being an Insane Clean Freak, my mom ironed every shred of ironable fabric in the house. Each week, regardless of whatever adolescent drama I was dealing with, I had four or five heaping plastic laundry baskets to iron. My brother Guy and I suffered the ultimate High School Humiliation: our ragged, patched jeans had perfectly centered, knife-edge creases.

Poor Little Kay, who was having a tough time with puberty to begin with, had to spend roughly twenty hours a week in the basement, ironing and muttering rude things about Mom. I hated it, I tell you.

Imagine my consternation when, one Christmas in my thirties, Mom gave me a steam iron. I could not believe that she did not see the rich irony in this so-called gift. But hey, she meant well. In the world of Insane Clean Freaks, this was the Holy Grail.

The iron Mom gave me was not just any iron. It was a Rowenta. A pricey European iron with all the bells and whistles. A yuppie iron, if you will. I did not understand why anybody who did not work in a laundry needed such an iron. But I took it home and plugged it in.

The scales fell from my eyes. Rowenta, "ich liebe dich!" I love your Germanic heft and solidity. I love that you do not emit wimpy steam puffs: You blast forth clouds of steam, like a mighty locomotive. You are Rowenta, hear you roar!

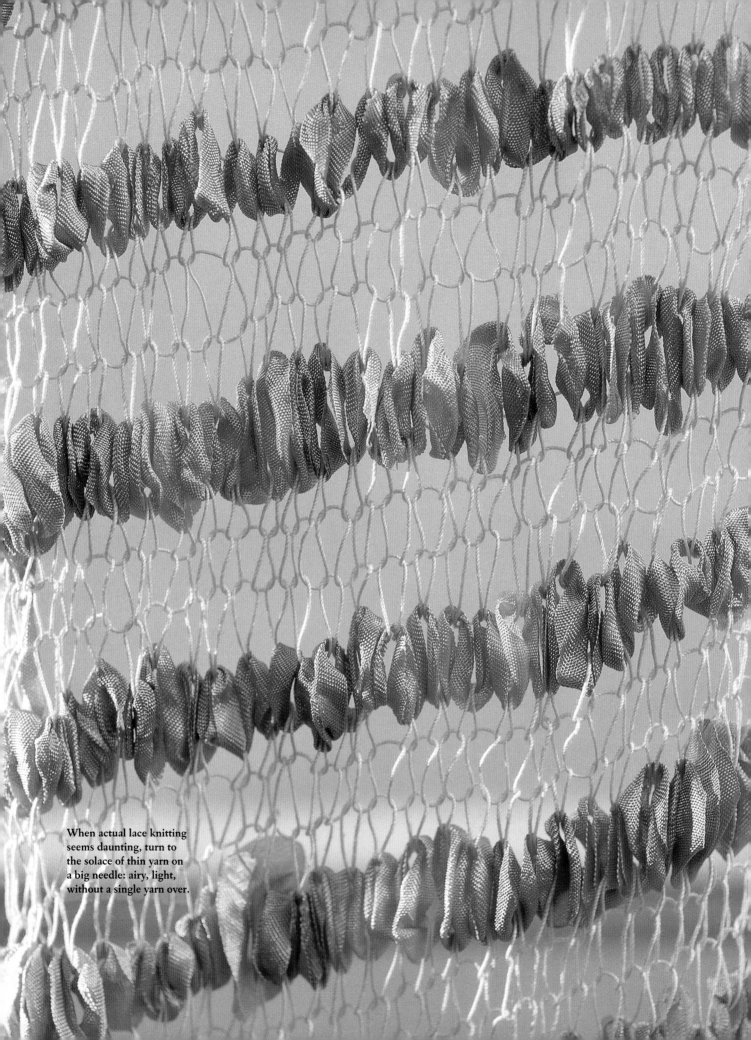

When actual lace knitting
seems daunting, turn to
the solace of thin yarn on
a big needle: airy, light,
without a single yarn over.

Ann

WHAT IF LE CORBUSIER TOOK TO KNITTING?

I keep thinking about Le Corbusier. You know, the twentieth-century architect with the round, black eyeglasses. Not Philip Johnson. No, not I. M. Pei. Le Corbusier was *le* French one, the Modernist who saw the potential in concrete. He made a lot of shockingly untraditional buildings out of this most humble of materials.

My senior year in college, I visited Notre Dame du Haut in Ronchamp in the countryside east of Paris. This chapel, finished in 1955 by Le Corbusier, sits on the site of a medieval church that was bombed during World War II. It looks so unlike a medieval church that only a careful inspection reveals that it contains any traditional church elements at all. The nave feels like a cavern; the stained glass punches through thick walls in no pattern; and the bells are not up in a tower—they're on a rack at ground level.

The other day, rooting around in my wallet for a yarn store frequent buyer card, I came across a souvenir I have carried around for almost twenty years. It's the ticket I was given when I paid my three francs to see the chapel. I have carried it with me all these years because the chapel at Ronchamp blew my mind. Whenever I look at that ticket, I think about that moment when I came up the hill, having seen the chapel only in black-and-white pictures in my mom's architecture book. Seeing it in real life was like that scene in *The Wizard of Oz* when they turn on the Technicolor.

That's what it was like when I first opened up Debbie New's *Unexpected Knitting*: Somebody turned on the lights. I thought I knew something about knitting, even in my amateur way. How wrong was I? Like our French friend of the round black glasses, Debbie New works with plain, ordinary materials. She's not knitting with gold, though she loves a luxurious mohair as much as Le Corbu loved a sleek granite. She uses all the same stitches you or I use: She knits, she purls, she embraces garter stitch. But her imagination is a wonder, and she lets it guide what happens with her knitting. She makes up her own sets of rules, based on her interest in mathematics or biology. She also sits down with a batch of beautiful yarn and simply knits, free-form, until she has a swirling vest that looks like a Tiffany window. It's an intuitive kind of knitting, and as far as I'm concerned, it's the most inspired, and inspiring, knitting I have seen.

I wanted to enter Debbie New's world. The simplest technique in New's book is one I want to share here, because it has given me enormous pleasure. Scribble lace knitting is a simple idea: Knit one row in a thick yarn, three rows in a very thin yarn. New makes all sorts of things out of scribble lace: a cardigan, a dress. For me, I'm happy making scribble lace as a simple panel, for a shawl or a throw; there is such fun in playing with yarn here that I don't need to go any further.

SHADE CARDS

★ ★ ★ ★ ★ ★ ★ ★ ★

KAY • It's official: You've Got it Bad when you break down and order a shade card. I first knew that my email friend Emma was a true blue forever friend when she sent me a binder of Rowan shade cards from the 1980s, just so I could see and touch the long-discontinued Mulberry Silk. When another email friend, Benedetta, came to New York and spent the night in my apartment, I woke up early the next day to find her sitting on the sofa in her PJs. Her knitting was tossed aside. She was staring into a binder: Emma's shade card.

Pawleys Scarf,
Weightless Scarf, and
Decayed Tutu Scarf:
theme and variation.

SCRIBBLING: THE BASIC RECIPE

Start with the notion of thick and thin. Your thick yarn can be as chunky as textile technology allows. The thin can go all the way down to sewing thread. If you follow this 8-row pattern, you will get a very cool effect. Be patient with the thin yarn—it can be tricky to work with a big needle, but soon enough you will be cranking out this stuff.

A: Thick yarn

B: Thin yarn

NEEDLES: Circulars are necessary even though this is knitted flat. Straight needles will not allow you to slide the stitches to the other end to make the single rows of thick yarn. The size is up to you, though anything smaller than a 15 (10mm) needle will likely diminish the openwork effect of the stitches. But don't let us get in your way.

Using A, very loosely CO 40 sts.

ROW 1: Join B. Knit.

ROW 2: Purl.

ROW 3: Knit.

ROW 4: Slide work to other end of circular needle. Carefully carry A up side of work. Using A, knit.

ROW 5: Using B, purl.

ROW 6: Knit.

ROW 7: Purl.

ROW 8: Slide work to other end of circular needle. Carefully carry A up side of work. Using A, purl.

Repeat these 8 rows until scarf is long enough to swish about in a dramatic way. Around 60" (152.5 cm) is usually good. Very loosely BO.

A FEW RECIPES

Pawleys Scarf

For summertime, when you're hot as hell but still require an accessory, this scarf is as decorative as it gets. I was amazed that this wacky yarn is mostly cotton—a novelty yarn in a natural fiber? I had to bite. The thin stuff is crochet thread.

SIZE: 16" x 60" (41 cm x 152.5 cm)
MATERIALS: Galaxy by Classic Elite, [1¾ oz (50g) ball, 83yds (75m), cotton/nylon] for color A
Cameo Craft Crochet, size 10 crochet cotton J.P. Coats, [each approx 350 yds (320 m), mercerized cotton] for color B
Size 17 (12.75 mm) needles
GAUGE: Doesn't matter!

Weightless Scarf

The goal with this scarf is to create something that has no weight but can keep you warm. Those mohair goats are onto something: Even though you can mail this scarf with just one first-class stamp, it is remarkably cozy. It can spread out to become a wrap, or, pulled from the ends, a scarf.

MATERIALS: Venezia by Lang, [1¾ oz (50g) ball, 142yds (130m), mohair/nylon]

one ball in teal for color A, Kid Silk Haze by Rowan Yarns, [.78oz (25g) ball, 229yds (210m), mohair/silk] one ball in teal for color B
Size 15 (10mm) circular needle
GAUGE: Doesn't matter!

Decayed Tutu Scarf

When I saw this Great Adirondack "½" Rayon Ribbon," it was clear to me that it was the most undernamed yarn in the world. ½" Rayon Ribbon? Surely not! How about Decayed Tutu, or Pavlova's Pointe Shoe Ribbons, or Sweepings from Degas's Workshop? I had to try it, and the results are lovely, if temperamental. Scribble lace works best with yarns that cling; a slippery yarn like this is prone to slide right out if snagged. But hey—ballet is all about beauty and pain, right?

SIZE: 14" x 48"
MATERIALS: ½" Rayon Ribbon by Great Adirondack for color A
Cameo Craft Crochet, size 10 crochet cotton J.P. Coats, [each approx 350 yds (320 m), mercerized cotton] for color B

Cotton yarn gives the
Nina shawl a fantastic
drape—so summery.

Ann

THE NINA SHAWL

Phyllis Howe is an original. She is simply one of those people who has *it*, that ineffable thing called style. Kay met Phyllis online, they started yakking, and before you know it, Kay is hanging out with Phyllis, knitting and carrying on. At some point Phyllis, in her typically stylish way, offered to host a sew-up bee for our Afghanalong charity knitting project (see Chapter 6, "Community Knitting") and the sew-up bee ended up being the place where Kay and I, after two years of e-mails, finally met in person. Aw.

On that epic day one September afternoon, a bunch of willing souls gathered in Phyllis's stylish New York townhouse to stitch up squares that had been sent from the four corners of the world. As we laid out the blankets and plotted what we would be sewing, Phyllis brought out a shawl she had made: a riot of color, in cotton, with a swingy drape and a ruffle at each end. It was fabulous. *Stylish!* She draped it across a chair beside the bounteous table of treats, and we all admired it in a covetous way.

Months later, I looked at the photos of the sew-up bee, and I was captivated by what Phyllis had done. Right there, next to the peach cobbler that Heather Lee had brought to the party via subway, was a study in the play of complement and contrast. The shawl uses four colors: orange, pink, black, and pale, pale green. The brights are such close cousins—hot pink and bright orange—that from a distance they read as one lush exclamation. The black and pale green make it vibrate, and the ruffle is pure sass. But look closer, and the pink and orange mess around with each other in a series of graduated stripes.

TOP REASONS TO USE SMALL NEEDLES

★ ★ ★ ★ ★ ★ ★ ★ ★ ★ ★

1
Cheap

You can knit for weeks on one skein of laceweight yarn—1,200 yards for the same price as 200 yards of worsted? Think about it.

2
Versatile

Finer-gauge knitted fabrics can be worn more often.

3
Complex

You can do amazing things in Fair Isle and intarsia if you knit smaller. The whole wide world opens up to you.

4
Confidence building

You will feel so very competent and grown up.

Sometimes a bit of *genius* shows up right next to the peach cobbler.

NINA SHAWL

By Phyllis Howe

Named for Phyllis's daughter, Nina provides the perfect framework to play with color. The rules are strict: Follow the stripe pattern, don't forget the checkerboard, and pay attention to how your colors contrast and complement. But beyond that, this handknit can morph from a cotton shawl to a mohair throw to a tweedy wrap.

SIZE: 60" x 24" (152.5 cm x 61 cm)

MATERIALS: Provence by Classic Elite, [3½ oz (100 g) hanks, each approx 205 yds (185 m), mercerized cotton]

A: hot pink 2 hanks

B: black 2 hanks

C: celadon 1 hank

D: orange 2 hanks

A DK weight wool or wool blend can easily be substituted

Size 6 (4 mm) needles or size needed to achieve gauge

GAUGE: 20 sts + 28 rows = 4" (10 cm) over St st.

Note: When cutting yarns, leave sufficient ends to be woven in when shawl is finished.

Using A, CO 120 sts.

For each row throughout pattern, k5 at beginning and end of each row to create garter stitch edge. The middle 110 stitches are worked in St st throughout pattern.

Work 12 rows. Cut A.

Join B. Work 2 rows.

Using the Fair Isle technique, in which the color not in use is carried loosely in back of work, begin the checkerboard pattern as follows:

ROW 1: Using B, k5. Join C. *k2 C, k2 B**. Continue from * to ** until last 5 sts. Using B, k5.

ROW 2: Purl, following the color pattern of Row 1.

ROW 3: Using B, k5. *k2 B, k2 C**. Continue from * to ** until last 5 stitches. Using B, k5.

ROW 4: Purl, following the color pattern of Row 3.

Repeat Rows 1-4 three more times to make 16 rows in checkerboard pattern. Using B, work 2 rows in St st. K4 rows. Cut B and C.

Join D. Work 2 rows. Do not cut yarn. Join A. Let D hang at the side while you use A to work 2 rows in St st. Switch to D and work 2 more rows in D. Alternate until you have completed 18 rows, ending with D. Cut D and A.

Join B. Work 4 rows. Cut B.

Join A. Work 6 rows. Cut A.

Join D. Work 6 rows. Cut D.

Join A. Work 6 rows. Cut A.

Join B. Work 4 rows. Cut B.

Join D. Work 9 rows. Cut D.

Join A. Work 9 rows. Cut A.

Join B. Work 4 rows. Cut B.

Join D. Work 18 rows. Cut D.

Join B. Work 4 rows. Cut B.

Join A. Work 18 rows. Cut A.

Join B. Work 18 rows. Cut B.

This is the halfway point on the shawl. Reverse all color and stripe patterns for the second half of the shawl. Work in reverse order until the last band of A. BO.

Ruffle

Starting on RS, using B, pick up 1 st in each st across. Purl 1 row. Knit 1 row. Purl 1 row.

Next row (RS): Inc 1 stitch 7 in each stitch across row.

Next row (WS): Purl. Continue in St st until 2" (5 cm) long. BO.

Make ruffle for other end of shawl.

Look what happens to the
Nina shawl when you
change the yarns: a total
mood change.

WHY WE SHOULD ALL KNIT LACE:
Emma Magnago-Prime

Now this is lace! Our Danish biotech engineer and lace-knitting friend, Thomas Holm, sent us this extraordinary Shetland shawl as a gift. We'd never seen such a fantastic combination of technical skill and artistry.

From her home on the edge of the Dales in a northeast coastal town in England, Emma Magnago-Prime has helped thousands of knitters all over the world see their knitting with a clear eye. Her prodigious circle of friends online look to Emma for her straightforward advice and "damn the torpedoes" attitude.

Q: I'm intrigued by what you say about "reading" your knitting—recognizing what those stitches are doing on those needles.

A: Reading your knitting does come more easily with experience. With texture, lace, and color patterns—if they're good—there's a rhythm that insinuates itself. You can get a bit of a Zen thing going, if you're lucky. The knitting is so pleasurable and easy when that happens. It sings a song. Combined with a beautiful yarn, what more could you want?

Reading lace is so easy. The pattern and flow echo the chart. You have to have confidence in your abilities and relax into it. Lace and cables are just knit and purl stitches whose order is changed. That's all!

Q: You're always tweaking your patterns. What's that all about?

A: Knitting is very like cooking. My mother-in-law has a very small repertoire of meals. They are repeated in the same sequence for years. If it's Monday, it's liver and bacon; Tuesday is gammon steak with chips. You can knit like that: the pattern as written, the yarn called for, even the same color as in the photo. But then you miss the pure joy of making the recipe/garment/pattern you own. Tweaking to taste, evolving an idea, reveling in colors that speak to you. Maybe you need a little bit of arrogance to do that—confidence in your abilities and taste. Just playing with color choices is so liberating. It isn't just that. It's the thirst for knowledge—wanting to find other, and better, ways to do things.

Q: What advice would you give to a new knitter?

A: My big bit of advice: Enjoy your knitting. It's only yarn! Revel in color and fiber. Be a little brave and arrogant, try new stuff and think outside the box.

THE QUEEN OF FINISHING:
Becky Delgado

Becky Delgado taught herself to knit. A corporate lawyer living in Lyon, France, she started her knitting blog (www.skinnyrabbit.com) to connect with knitters who shared her fixation. She combined her love of knitting and a freakish ability to crank computer code to launch Pretty Posies, a Web-hosting service for knitting bloggers. The grand hostess of hostesses, Becky provides an online home to dozens of knitters. She is also the subject of awe as the Patron Saint of Finishing.

Q: When I first came across Fluffa!, your web site, I was knocked out by many things: your headless dancing shots, your Boy, but most of all the relish you show for the task most knitters loathe—finishing. Surely, there is no more fiendish finishing junkie than you. How did this happen? What led you to the point that you would, um, track down four shades of embroidery floss so that the seams are sewn in the same shade as the stripes?

A: I've been anal-retentive (OK, a perfectionist) since birth. Let's skip back to the seventies when I was . . . well, a heckuva lot younger than I am now. When I'd color in my coloring books, I'd first outline everything with a shade darker than I intended to color, and then I'd fill in ever

A Beckyish moment: Ann embroiders a label.

so carefully. Why? Because I couldn't have one single bit of color go out of the lines.

I should have known back then that this was a foreshadowing of my fiendish finishing in knitting, and everything else. If something doesn't come out the way I like, I'll keep fixing it until it does. A crooked seam? I'll twitch. Must rip out and straighten it! Holes when I picked up stitches for a neckband? I'll blink furiously, and then rip out and pick up until the holes vanish. I enjoy the process of knitting, but I further enjoy the near-perfect results that I know can be achieved through meticulous finishing. Finishing should be handled like a good gourmet meal. Don't rush through it! Savor it. Knitting is cool, but finishing is what can make you especially proud of your completed work.

Chapter Six

COMMUNITY*KNITTING

EVERY ONCE IN A WHILE, OVER THE YEARS

I've been knitting,

I GET THE YEN TO FIND A

CIRCLE

OF*KNITTERS,

and Belong Unto It.

Kay ✳ One of the pleasures of knitting is that it is solitary, complete in itself. There's no need to write it down in your calendar or call anybody on the phone. You don't need a partner, or a foursome, and the weather doesn't matter, either. There's no need to buy supplies or specialized equipment (because you already own all the yarn, needles and pattern books your home can possibly hold). You grab an hour, a spot on the sofa, and a favorite cuppa, and you're in business.

Alone with your knitting, your mind can wander gently among your thoughts, only occasionally having to come back to count rows. The needles in your hands go clickety-click. Some part of your brain notices, with quiet enjoyment, the quirks of the yarn you're using, while another part gains an ever-deeper understanding of the stitch pattern. The television natters on, politely, as British detectives solve another of the violent murders that are such a plague upon the quaint rural towns of England. The project grows. This is Enough. You love it just like this. You don't need anything more.

And then you go, Hey! I'm lonely! I'm sitting here drinking tea and knitting BY MYSELF. That's PATHETIC!

THE SEARCH FOR A CIRCLE

Every once in a while, over the years I've been knitting, I get the yen to find a circle of knitters, and Belong Unto It. Stopping by the local yarn store, I see a group of women around the table, chatting and knitting. Laughing and ripping out. Giving each other unsolicited advice. What fun! I want to squeeze in and knit for a while, but I'm afraid. They seem like such a cozy unit. They don't seem to need a new face. The knitting in my bag looks simpleminded and dull compared to the projects these Knitting Store Regulars are knitting. (Why did I have to bring the dishcloth, today of all days?) They are Fair-Isling in the round. They are yarn-overing all over. And talking at the same time. Wistfully, I pay for my stuff and leave.

In my longing for knitting pals, I gravitated toward the Internet. First, the Rowan message board, which often seems like a virtual knitting circle. You post a comment to someone's comment or question, and somebody else responds almost immediately to what you just said. The conversation is more or less related to Rowan patterns and yarns, which everybody on the board adores. It's fun. After a while, I felt, weirdly, like I knew some of these women. We'd get each other's e-mail addresses, and sometimes we'd start corresponding privately, like old-fashioned pen pals. That's how I "met" Ann, after all. That's how I "met" Polly and Yvonne, Emma and Benedetta. After a while I knew the names of husbands, children, pets, what sweater they were working on, what they did for a living. I also felt as if I knew who they were. This was before many people were blogging, so there were no "100 Things About Me"

SEW-UP BEES The Afghanalong Sew-Up Bees were the exception to the rule that sewing-up sucks.

to snoop through. I had to piece people together from the tidbits they shared.

But it was bound to happen sooner or later: a chance to meet. In person. To sit in the same room with one of them, or a bunch of them. Freaky! Not sure I liked the idea. I felt afraid, as I had felt afraid of those cozy groups in the yarn store.

On an Internet chat board, if you don't speak up on a regular basis, people don't know you're there. To exist, you have to say something. So it can be disconcerting to meet an Internet friend in person; the chattiest person on the Web can turn out to be serene, even tongue-tied, in the flesh. Polly was not tongue-tied, but she was very soft-spoken. That first meeting, we had a lovely, quiet knit over a cup of coffee, and our conversation did not range beyond knitting. We bought yarn together—the knitterly equivalent of smoking the peace pipe. I returned home to Hubby, who was glad that Polly wasn't an Internet ax murderer who had lured me, with yarn and marmalade, to an untimely death. (Can you tell that Hubby reads the *New York Post?*)

I have met Polly many times since then, once on a trip to London, but usually on one of her trips to visit her parents, who live in New York. Somehow, Polly has been transformed from a name on my screen to an actual friend. A very good actual friend. The kind of friend who sends you a Christmas pudding, whose calling card is a jar of marmalade. The kind of friend who knits twenty squares for your charity project. The kind of friend who, when she came to New York to bury her beloved grandmother, put her husband on the subway with two giant shopping bags of yarn she had bought for me in the semi-annual Rowan sale at Liberty of London. That yarn was Holy Yarn. It was Friendship Yarn.

KNITTING FOR THE COMMON GOOD

After you've been knitting for a while, another urge hits you: to knit for the Common Good. As knitting becomes more deeply ingrained in your soul, you begin to think that knitting for another human being is the best way to express love, concern, and solidarity. It starts with gifts. You hear that a friend's father has passed away; you know she is hurting. She is far away from you, so you can't take her a tuna casserole or sit with her in her living room. So you knit her a scarf in a precious, indulgent yarn. This scarf seems to express your condolence better than mere words.

After gifts for loved ones comes the urge to knit for strangers in need. To a non-knitter, the idea of knitting hats for the homeless, or booties for premature babies, may seem like an insignificant drop in the bucket of the world's need. Why knit for people when, clearly, it would be more efficient simply to send a monetary contribution and let a charitable organization buy commercially made clothing for those who are cold? But we knitters know better. We believe that, somehow, the tiniest baby or his worried mother, or a homeless person with stark needs and dulled senses, can be cheered by the work of our hands. That they will receive not just the warmth of the item, but an additional benefit from the knowledge (conscious or unconscious) that a friendly stranger made it with her hands.

I started looking for a project to pour my knitting love into. I learned of many wonderful organizations of knitters who knit Christmas caps and scarves for merchant seamen; blankets, hats, and gloves for the poor; and even, heartbreakingly, burial gowns for stillborn infants. If I get enough knitting time in my life, I hope to knit for all of them. But the one that first grabbed me was an organization called Afghans for Afghans.

A hodgepodge of squares from all over the globe, transformed into beautiful blankets.

THE AFGHANALONG

Afghan-a-Long

The knitting club invites you to join them in sewing together squares to make afghans for refugees in Afghanistan. The sewing party will be from 10:00 to 2:00 on Wednesday, Nov. 10th in the AC room.

In February 2004, we made an announcement on Mason-Dixon Knitting: We were seeking knitted squares to be sewn into blankets. The blankets would be sent to Afghans for Afghans, a charity in California that delivers handknits, new clothing, and blankets to displaced people in Afghanistan. To make it more fun, we would draw names every month for a bag of deluxe yarn (most of which had been lugged, by Polly, across the Atlantic from the Liberty sale). At the end of six months of collecting squares, we would host Old-Timey Sew-Up Bees in New York and Nashville. Anybody who could get there was invited to come over, meet online pals, eat some Cheetos (the official salty snack of Mason-Dixon Knitting), and sew blankets together.

At the start, I was nervous. How embarrassing if we didn't get even the forty squares or so that a single blanket would take. It would be like throwing a very public party, inviting the world, laying in bales of Cheetos, and nobody showing up.

But of course that didn't happen. These are knitters, remember? They did not let us down. The squares started to roll in. Logging and snapping pictures of them to post on the blog became a substantial part-time job. The monthly report and updating of the map showing the states and countries from which squares had come became our favorite feature.

By the end of the Afghanalong, we had collected over one thousand squares from more than two hundred knitters, in forty states and thirteen countries, and made twenty-five gorgeous patchwork blankets. There were Old-Timey Sew-up Bees not just in New York and Nashville, but at the homes of generous knitters in Chicago, Toronto, Montreal, Denver, and Boston.

The whole experience was, for lack of a better word, gobsmacking. Humbling. And really fun.

Was it the most efficient way to get warm blankets to Afghanistan? No. (We spent as much time blogging about it as making squares.) Was it the fastest way to help? No. (It took us almost a year to make blankets that would warm a few families.) Was it the cheapest way? No. (Think of the postage!) But for those who participated, it made the world seem smaller, and the people in it more connected to each other. And we hope the blankets, which plainly are products of many skilled hands working together, will be appreciated by the recipients in a way that a mass-produced covering could never be.

To our surprise, we got enough squares made of glorious, self-striping Noro yarns to make this all-Noro blanket. It had to be pried out of Kay's hands to be sent off to the high bidder in an eBay auction. The proceeds were donated to Afghans for Afghans to help underwrite their cost of delivering blankets and clothing on chartered planes.

A SQUARE FOR AFGHANISTAN, FROM AFGHANISTAN

The Highest Mileage Award goes to one cheerful dishcloth cotton square. Tish Dudevoir decided we needed to have at least one square that came from Afghanistan. From her home in West Point, New York, Tish sent the square she made to her sister Jenny Caruso, an Army lieutenant colonel who was stationed in Afghanistan. Jenny received it, then promptly returned it to the States, postmarked Kabul. After being sewn into an afghan, the square returned to Kabul: a total voyage of 20,200 miles (32,501km).

A gang of baby-crazy knitters can pile up the bibs and burpies in sufficient quantity for the drooliest, burpiest infant.

This shower concept is not for your *fancy-shmancy* pal

SHOWER THE BABIES YOU LOVE WITH HANDKNITS

A knitter who is expecting a baby is the ideal victim, er, target, er, special guest of a group-knitting baby shower. Let's be clear: This shower concept is *not* for your fancy-shmancy pal who has registered for the Burberry diaper bag and the Louis Vuitton messy-mat. Although a mom-to-be who is herself a knitter can best appreciate the love, time, and attention that goes into a handknit layette, everyone but the most logo-conscious woman would cherish a collection of squooshy hand-knits for her precious newborn.

Organizing this kind of knitting for a group is tricky. The items to be knit must be accessible to knitters of different levels of skill, and ideally, they should be quick enough to knit so that the hostess of the shower doesn't have to call people up and beg them to finish their items before the baby starts high school. They should also be composed, for the most part, of TV-knitting, so that people can enjoy the party while they knit.

With this in mind, our baby shower items are, in the main, garter-stitch festivals. Yet cute. Yet funky. Yet fun.

Why did we make three layettes in three different yarns? We did it for you, Dear Reader. We did it to give you options.

COST. If you make the Peaches & Creme version, you can literally make the whole layette for the price of a Baby Bjorn.

COLORFASTNESS. Peaches & Creme is pure cotton, and it is both soft and durable. It fades, though. Some shades fade a lot. We're very comfortable with burp cloths, towels, bibs, and washcloths fading. Fading is part of their charm as everyday objects. But if you're not comfortable with fading, use a premium cotton yarn.

THE BOY OPTION. All three versions are suitable for boys or girls. (The kids nowadays are so unisex.) But if you want to do a super-boyish version, choose the Rowan Denim. It is designed to both shrink and fade, so we've added a few rows to the patterns. In a short time, they will look like James Dean's old blue jeans, and of course, they will go with the rest of a baby boy's wardrobe, which is likely to skew markedly toward blue. You can decorate them with patches from the local fire and police departments or vintage merit badges.

who has registered for the Burberry diaper bag.

Denim on a baby girl . . . awww!

BABY BIB O' LOVE

SIZE: 6½" x 11½" (16.5 cm x 29 cm)

MATERIALS: Handknit Cotton by Rowan Yarns, [1¾ oz (50 g) balls, each approx 93 yds (85 m), cotton] or Denim by Rowan Yarns [1¾ oz (50 g) balls, each approx 102 yds (93 m), cotton] or Peaches & Creme worsted weight by Elmore-Pisgah Inc., [solid colors 2½ oz (71.5 g) balls, each approx 122yds (112m) cotton], or 95 yds (87 m) of any DK weight cotton yarn.

Size 6 (4 mm) needles

GAUGE: It doesn't really matter! Approx 20 sts + 40 rows = 4" (10 cm) over garter st.

CO 40 sts.

NEXT AND ALL ROWS: Knit.

Continue until you have 32 garter ridges (64 rows), or if using Rowan Denim, 36 garter ridges.

NEXT ROW: Begin the neck straps. K10,

CO 20 sts, k final 10 sts. Leave first 10 sts on needle to be knitted later. Turn work, k10 sts until strap is 5" (12.5 cm) long. BO.

Return to the 10 sts being held on needle and make the second strap. K10 until strap is 4" (10 cm). Make a buttonhole in the following manner: K4, BO 2, k4. Next row: K4, CO 2 using backward loop method, k4. Or use whatever buttonhole method you like. Next row: Knit. Continue knitting until second strap matches the first in length. BO. Sew on button. Decorate bib if you're so inclined.

Repeat. Make a bunch of 'em. Babies are a mess!

BABY GENIUS BURP CLOTHS

Studies have proven that babies who spit up onto burp cloths that display interesting textures, patterns, and colors, do better on their SATs than babies who spit up onto plain white diapers or bare shoulders. The Ivy League is getting more competitive every year. Seventeen years from now, they may be admitting only two kids. Give that special baby an edge: Get knitting!

SIZE: Approx 7" x 10" (18 cm x 25.5 cm)

MATERIALS: Handknit Cotton by Rowan Yarns [1¾ oz (50 g) balls, each approx 93 yds (85 m), cotton] or Denim by Rowan Yarns [1¾ oz (50 g) balls, each approx 102 yds (93 m), cotton] or Peaches & Creme worsted weight by Elmore-Pisgah Inc., [solid colors 2½ oz (71.5 g) balls, each approx 122yds (112m) cotton], or 95 yds (87 m) of any DK weight cotton yarn.

GAUGE: Doesn't matter. This is a burp cloth. Fit is not an issue.

Solid Version

CO 50 sts.

ROW 1 (WS–YES, IT'S WEIRD FOR THE FIRST ROW TO BE ON THE WRONG SIDE, BUT IT IS): K2, *p1, k4; rep from * to last 3 sts, p1, k2.

ROW 2 (RS): K2, *sl 1 purlwise with yarn in back, k4; rep from * to last 3 sts, slip 1 purlwise with yarn in back, k2.

Repeat these 2 rows 60 more times, or 70 more if you are using Rowan Denim, then repeat Row 1 one more time. BO.

Stripe Version

Note: For this version, use 2 colors of your chosen yarn, A and B.

Using A, CO 50 sts.

ROW 1 (WS): K2, *p1, k4; rep from * to last 3 sts, k1, k2.

ROW 2 (RS): Join B. (Do not cut A.) K2, *sl 1 purlwise with yarn in back, k4; rep from * to last 3 sts, sl 1 purlwise with yarn in back, k2.

ROW 3: K2, *p1, k4, rep from * to last 3 sts, p1, k2.

Continue to work 2 rows using A and 2 rows using B throughout.

Repeat Rows 2 and 3 sixty more times, or seventy more times if are using Rowan Denim, ending with a WS row. BO.

You can gussy up plain bibs with appliqués, embroidery, or vintage merit badges. The days of the week? Baby's initials? I HEART UNCLE BOB? Go to it!

Gauge variation?
We're not scared of
gauge variation! This
blanket proves that
three is not a crowd.

A KEEPSAKE BLANKET KNIT BY THREE FRIENDS

Sometimes you want to make sure that your baby gift is going to make the mother-to-be burst into tears of uncontrollable joy. Our research has revealed that the best way to achieve this objective is for three friends to get together and knit a one-of-a-kind blanket that is imbued with meaningful symbols. A blanket that is vibrating with love and hope for a new baby's happiness in life. If you make this blanket, you and your friends can sit back, relax, and enjoy the baby shower: The mom-to-be's tears are 100 percent guaranteed.

OK, so that's not really the story of this blanket. While I do occasionally get the slightest bit competitive about winning the coveted Cutest Handmade Baby Gift Award, this blanket was never opened up at a baby shower. It's another Internet Knitting Love Story.

I "met" Cristina through Mason-Dixon Knitting. When we started the Afghanalong, she was one of the first to send in squares. (I know this because there is her name, Cristina B. Shiffman, on the very first page of the Afghanalong log book.) Cristina sent in squares every month, for all six months of the Afghanalong. At the time I was getting to know her, she had one son, age six. Midway through the Afghanalong, she shared with us that she was expecting another son, around Thanksgiving.

In early November, I boarded a train in Penn Station, heading for Philly, to meet Cristina. Cristina had, due to the fatigue of the third trimester of pregnancy, missed our Afghanalong sew-up bee in New York. So she convened a mini-sew-up at her house. The exclusive guest list was me and Cristina's real-life pal Cheryl.

Cristina's house was a child-friendly haven of peace, art, and chocolate. As I always do my first time in a knitter's home, I asked to be taken on the Fiber Arts Tour. There, on the wall over her son's bed, was a handmade quilt to which every female member of Cristina's family had contributed a square. At the top of the stairs, beautifully framed, was a piece of abstract appliqué art that one of Cristina's sisters, a textile artist, had made.

Cheryl drove me to the train station to go home. As we got in her car, I was bursting with a plan for Cheryl, Ann, and me to make this blanket for Cristina's new baby. This was going to be one handknit blanket that would be appreciated by the recipient.

WE'VE LEARNED TWO THINGS FROM ANTIQUES ROADSHOW: Never, ever, refinish a piece of furniture, and provenance is everything. Take the time to duplicate-stitch personal details on the finished blanket.

KEEPSAKE BLANKET

A totally addicting project. There are only a few rules: Everybody uses the same yarn. Although there is always a slight gauge variation when different knitters are working different stitch patterns, everybody knits a panel that is roughly the same size. Beyond that, anything goes. We found that even Ann's ridiculously textured stitch choices somehow found a home in a blanket like this. The whole thing is a riot of pattern and texture, reflecting the curiosity of each knitter, but it is harmonized by using the same yarn and palette. If you have been wary of trying new stitch patterns that look complicated, this is the place to try them. We encourage adventurous experimentation. But even if everyone knits nothing but garter stitch, this blanket will be richly beautiful.

SIZE: Finished blanket is approx 44" x 64" (111.5 cm x 162.5 cm). Each panel is 12" x 60" (30.5 cm x 152 cm)

MATERIALS: Denim by Rowan Yarns, [1¾ oz (50 g) balls, each approx 102 yds (93 m), cotton]. Each panel uses approx 2 balls each of light blue, medium blue and dark indigo, and 1 ball ecru. The outer border and inner connection strips, as shown in the photograph, use

A denim blanket will show its age gracefully. The baby grows; the blanket fades.

DA MIBASIA MILLE

ELIO NATALE·12·10·04

6 balls ecru.

Size 6 (4 mm) needles or size needed to achieve gauge

Size 6 (4 mm) circular needle, 60" (150 cm) long

GAUGE: 20 sts + 28 rows = 4" (10 cm) over St st.

TO MAKE A PANEL: CO 60 sts. Knit in your chosen stitch patterns until your panel is 60" (152.5 cm). BO.

In our blanket, you'll see garter stitch, stockinette, seed stitch, basketweave, reverse stockinette ticking stripes, cables, panels, gansey stitch patterns. We used a lot of patterns from Barbara Walker's *Second Treasury of Knitting Patterns*, including Shadow Rib, Dimple Stitch, Snowball Stitch, Dragon Skin, and Pilsener Pleating.

Joining

Arrange the panels as desired. With a 60" (150 cm) circular needle and ecru, pick up stitches along the right edge of the first panel, using a ratio of approximately 2 stitches picked up per 3 row ends of the edge. Work these stitches in moss stitch for 12 rows. Leave them on the needle. With another long circular needle and another ball of ecru, pick up stitches along the left edge of the second panel, and cut the yarn. Now, with right sides facing each other, join these two pieces by working a 3-needle bind-off. Repeat to join third panel.

Border

With a 60" (150 cm) circular needle and ecru, pick up stitches along one of the outer edges of the blanket. For cast-on and bound-off edges, pick up one stitch in each edge stitch. For selvedge edges, use a ratio of approx 2 stitches picked up per 3 rows. Moss st for 11 rows, ending with a WS row. At the same time, increase one stitch at each end of every RS row by knitting into the front and back of the first and last stitch. Bind off in moss st on the RS. Repeat on the remaining 3 edges. Join the border at the corners using mattress stitch.

Kaycam

GO YOUR OWN WAY
The fun of this blanket is that each knitter can do her own thing. The rules are few. The soft blues of the denim yarn ensure harmony, no matter how deeply you go into your Barbara Walkers.

TECHNICAL HINT

Three-needle Bind-off ★ Place the two needles holding the edges to be joined in your left hand. With a third (straight) needle, join the two pieces by knitting into one stitch from each needle at the same time, and binding off the stitches as in a normal bind-off. Ideally, you have exactly the same number of stitches on both edges. If not, you need to sometimes knit 1 stitch from one needle together with 2 stitches from the other needle, evenly spaced along the row of stitches, so that at the end of the row, you bind off the last stitch from each needle at the same time.

A Moses Basket quickly becomes a cherished memento of a newborn who is growing fast. The lining can be saved for the next baby, but the basket also makes a lovely container for toys and memorabilia.

BIRTH OF A COZY

ow let us speak of heirlooms. What has happened to heirlooms? I'm not talking about silver tea sets, old Victrolas, or the Christmas china. I'm talking about cutwork tablecloths and candlewick bedspreads—the stuff people used to inherit from Grandma and keep in a cedar chest.

The problem is: The grandmas of today sort of dropped that ball. We're not mad at them or anything. They were out burning their bras and marching for the Equal Rights Amendment. They bowled, they danced, they made a lot of very interesting 1970s pottery, and they traveled all over creation. They were busy being the exact opposite of what grandmas used to be. They did not do a lot of needlework.

Whatever the cause, the tradition of passing down handmade textiles has died down, and by cracky, it is up to us, the knitters of today, to raise it up again. But how? We could replicate the heirlooms of the past, but these intricate, old-fashioned things look musty and froofy to our eyes. Instead, we should make things that we love today, with clean lines and simple patterns, in beautiful yarns that will last.

I was thinking about the Heirlooms of Tomorrow when the idea of a Moses basket cozy occurred to me. When a new baby comes into my family or circle of close friends, I feel an overwhelming urge to make something precious and lasting. In many churchgoing families, exquisite christening gowns, either handmade by an ancestor or bearing the label of a long-defunct fancy department store, are passed down from generation to generation. I wanted to make something with a similar ability to be used at the special time when a baby is new, and then be passed down, appearing in the family album over and over.

One day I saw a wee bairn in an elegant Madison Avenue boutique Moses basket. What is a Moses basket, anyway, but a Baby Display Device? You have a new baby. You want to show off your new baby. What your baby needs, my friend, is a kickass Moses basket.

In knitting, as in life, there are usually two ways to go: The easy way and the hard way. Often we find out about the easy way only when we are three-quarters of the way through with the hard way. That is what happened to me with the Moses basket.

My first vision was of a basket lined completely with linen. In other words, a Moses basket cozy. The outside edging begins with four equal-length strips of Peasant Ruffle from *Knitting on the Edge*, Nicky Epstein's book on knitted trims. This dramatic border is perfect for a first lace project because it is an easily memorized repeat of a few stitches over only two rows. When the border pieces are finished, they are joined and you continue in the round, making openings for the handles that are exactly like the one-row buttonholes you would make for a cardigan, but twenty-seven stitches wide. When you reach the top of the basket, you decrease the number of stitches so that the lining will fit the inside of the basket. Then you knit a few more inches/centimeters of stockinette stitch, and you're done. While this may look like a large project, it takes only four skeins of yarn to line the basket completely. And when you think about it, is four skeins too high a price for immortality?

MOSES BASKET, AMBITIOUS GRANDMOTHER VERSION

You can purchase a Moses basket at most baby furnishings stores. Make sure that the basket does not have an attached hood. This basket that came with simple, white cotton padding inside and over the top edge, which was ideal for supporting the knitted lining. Choose a basket that does not have ruffles or other embellishments that will prevent the lining from lying smoothly.

MATERIALS: Euroflax Originals sport weight by Louet Sales, [3½ oz (100 g) hanks, each approx 270 yds (247 m), linen] 4 hanks in pink

Approx ½ yd (.5 m) of cotton fabric (for bottom of the basket; you may be able to use the fabric liner that comes with the basket)

Size 5 (3.75 mm) circular needle, at least

29" (73.5 cm) long

Stitch markers in 3 colors or types

GAUGE: 20 sts + 32 rows = 4" (10 cm) over St st.

Lace Ruffle (make 4)

Using straight needles, CO 210 sts.

ROW 1 (RS): K1, *SKP, yo twice, k2tog; rep from * to last st, k1.

ROW 2: P1, *p1, (p1, k1) in yo, p1; rep from * to last st, p1.

Repeat these two rows 11 times.

NEXT (DEC) ROW: K2tog across the row (105 sts).

Leave these stitches on a spare circular needle.

When you have all 4 ruffles on your

circular needle, join, place a marker at the start of the first round, and work in the round as follows:

Work 8 rnds seed st.

Work 8 rnds St st.

NEXT ROUND (Set up round for decreases; new markers should be distinguishable from the marker already placed at start of round): Slip marker, k105, pm, k105, pm, k105, pm, k105 (420 sts).

NEXT ROUND (Set up round for seed st handle openings; new markers should be distinguishable from markers already placed): Slip marker, k33, pm, work in seed st for 39 sts, pm, k33, sl marker, k105, sl marker, k33, pm, work in seed st for 39 sts, pm, k33, sl marker, k105.

Repeat the previous row 5 times.

NEXT ROW (make openings for handles): K33, work 5 sts in seed st, BO 29 sts in seed st, work 5 sts in seed st, kl71, work 5 sts in seed stitch, BO 29 sts in seed st, work 5 sts in seed st, k138.

NEXT ROW: K33, work 5 sts in seed st, CO 29 sts over the sts bound off in prev row, work 5 sts in seed st, kl71, work 5 sts in seed stitch, CO 29 sts over the sts bound off in prev row, work 5 sts in seed st, k138.

NEXT ROW (dec and placing two additional markers): K1, k2tog, k30, work in seed st for 39 sts, k31, ssk, k1, k2tog, k47, ssk, pm, k1, k2tog, k48, ssk, k1, k2tog, k30, work in seed st for 39 sts, k31, ssk, k1, k2tog, k47, ssk, pm, k1, k2tog, k48, ssk (408 sts).

NEXT ROW: Work even, working the 39 stitches of seed st over the handle openings.

NEXT (DEC) ROW: Work all stitches as

before, decreasing 1 stitch before and after each marker as in the previous decrease round, including the marker that indicates the start of the round (396 sts).

NEXT ROW: Work even.

NEXT (DEC) ROW: K every stitch, removing the markers previously placed before and after the 39 sts of moss st, and slipping all other markers, and working decreases before and after each marker as set (384 sts).

NEXT ROW: Knit every stitch.

Repeat the previous two rows 3 more times (348 sts).

Work in St st for approx 8" (20 cm), or until the lining is long enough to reach the bottom of the basket (check frequently, as baskets vary).

The only trick to this Moses basket is putting the handle openings and shaping decreases in the right spots. Use different markers for each purpose so you don't get confused.

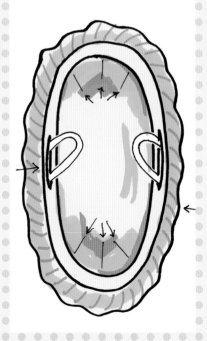

Finishing

Sew the four strips of the ruffle together using mattress stitch, and weave in ends. To install the liner in the basket securely: If the basket came with a fabric liner that you are not using, cut the bottom portion away from the rest of the lining. Pin or baste the bottom edge of the knitted lining all the way around this fabric bottom. Make sure that you align the 3 decreases on either end of the knitted lining with the curved ends of the basket. Take care to pin or baste the knitted lining evenly so that it will not bunch or gap. After testing it by placing it in the basket, whipstitch the knitted lining to the fabric bottom.

Blocking

Place the lining in the basket, smooth it inside and along the edge, and dampen it lightly with a spray bottle. Let it dry. Then, using a steamer or an iron that will steam vertically, steam the liner, pulling on the lace as you go to open it up and straighten the edge.

Put in the mattress that came with the basket, insert adorable baby, and take a picture. It doesn't get any cuter than this.

YOU KNIT FOR ME, I'LL KNIT FOR YOU

★ ★ ★ ★ ★ ★ ★ ★ ★ ★ ★ ★ ★

ANN • Early in our correspondence, Kay had a brilliant idea: a knitting exchange. She would knit for me a pattern that I picked out, using whatever yarn I supplied. I would do the same for her. There was genius in this scheme. Whenever I make a sweater for myself, I am acutely aware of its imperfections. Even if I love it, I can show you the weird part of the sleeve seam. It's like working in the baloney factory—once you know how it's made, it's not quite as tasty. But a present? I'm thrilled to get a sweater that someone else made for me.

Knitting for Kay meant that I was on best behavior, because I knew she was a good knitter. No shortcuts. I even frogged half a sleeve because I wanted her sleeve to be just so. If it had been my sleeve, it would have been just not so.

If you have a friend who knits, do an exchange, and you'll end up with a sweater you know you'll love.

A KINDER, GENTLER MOSES BASKET

After taking a good hard look at the instructions for the Moses basket cozy, I started to worry. Using four skeins of sportweight linen, it is a fair stretch of knitting. Maybe, I thought, the only knitters who would make it would be those ultramotivated knitters on a mission from God: first-time grandmothers. And if I was right about that, what about all those second grandbabies out there? Could I just stand by and let them do their looking-adorable routine while lying in Moses baskets adorned by *machine-made ruffles*?

I did exhaustive research on behalf of the second grandbabies. With heroic effort, I reached up on my bookshelf and pulled down Barbara Walker's *Second Treasury of Knitting Patterns.* I flipped through "Edgings" until I got to "Godmother's Edging." How could you not use something called "Godmother's Edging" for a baby's basket? Especially after Barbara Walker tells us that it "was designed in the 1890s for the hems of infants' christening-dresses and matching lace cushions."

This simple basket will take only a few evenings of knitting while dreaming about new babies. It will also take only a skein and a half of Euroflax Originals Sportweight 100 percent linen yarn. I knitted most of this one (in less than a week) riding around on the subway doing my errands.

Godmother's Edging is an ideal first lace project. The pattern is self-correcting; if you make an error, you will notice it right away, in that very row, instead of many rows later when you look at your work. Because it is so easy to detect and correct mistakes, it is stress-free knitting.

How could you not use something called "*godmother's*

Waking up at three A.M. to feed your adorable heir, you think, Is that Moses basket covered in knitting? Impossible. I must be delirious.

edging" for a baby's basket?

Godmother's Edging is simple and elegant, and a heckuva lot easier than it looks. Can you count? Can you do a yarn over? You can do it.

MOSES BASKET, STOVETOP VERSION

This is a great portable project, and the most painless way to get comfortable with knitting lace.

MATERIALS: Euroflax Originals sport weight by Louet Sales, [3½ oz (100 g) hanks, each approx 270 yds (247 m), linen] 2 hanks in pale blue
Ready-made Moses basket with plain fabric liner, as shown in the photograph
Size 5 (3.75 mm) needles

GAUGE: Doesn't matter as long as you are not knitting so tightly that the lace pattern doesn't show.

CO 20 sts and knit one row.

ROW 1: Sl 1, k3, [yo, k2tog] 7 times, yo, k2 (21 sts).

ROWS 2, 4, 6, AND 8: Knit.

ROW 3: Sl 1, k6, [yo, k2tog] 6 times, yo, k2 (22 sts).

ROW 5: Sl 1, k9, [yo, k2tog] 5 times, yo, k2 (23 sts).

ROW 7: Sl 1, k12, [yo, k2tog] 4 times, yo, k2 (24 sts).

ROW 9: Sl 1, k23.

ROW 10: BO 4, k19 (20 sts).

Repeat rows 1-10 until you have four pieces in the correct lengths to fit around the basket liner, binding off at the end of each piece. (Because of the handles, you need 2 longer pieces to go between the handles, and 2 shorter pieces that fit in the gaps under the handles.) BO all stitches.

Note: Some Moses baskets will work with a single long strip of lace.

Finishing

Wash and machine-dry the strips, as specified on the yarn label, until they are barely damp. Steam the knitted strips to open up the lace and make the points even. Sew the edging neatly to the liner. (*Tip*: Split the Euroflax, which is 4 plies, to 2 plies, and use this matching thread for sewing up.)

NOW **THAT'S** A KNITTING CIRCLE
The Women of Revitz House

KAY • I took the Metro from Washington, D.C.'s Union Station, arriving at Revitz House, a Maryland apartment residence for seniors, at noon. The assembled Knitting Club had been working on the afghans since 10 A.M., making great progress. I was an object of great curiosity. I received a thorough inspection. According to Ancient Hebrew Custom, we ate Chinese food for lunch. I had brought a chocolate babka from New York, which was greeted with many swoons and sighs before being sliced, tasted, and wrapped in napkins to save for later. Then the Sewing Up resumed for the rest of the afternoon. The KayCam was there:

Dora
Dora made the striped lavender pullover she is wearing. Fine gauge. Lovely.

Gloria
Modeling my hand-knit jacket in Rowan Denim. It fits her perfectly. She wants me to make her one. She really wants me to make her one. She made that very clear.

Freida
Having spent many years working in New York's Garment District for well-known design houses, Freida was kind of overquali-fied for whip-stitching squares together, but she did not let that stop her. She fondly reminisced about her days in the city she calls "my New York," with empha-sis on the West 30s and Forest Hills in Queens. This started everyone else shar-ing their childhood memories.

Renee
Renee told about how she used to save the seven cents she was given (five cents for the subway and two cents for a bus transfer) by walk-ing to school from the West 90s, across Central Park, and all the way over to Lexington in the 60s. Renee has had several careers, including one in jewelry design.

Pearl
Pearl knit more squares for the Afghanalong than anybody else. Not just anybody else at Revitz House. Anybody else.

EPILOGUE

Epilogue? The End? Huh?

We were just getting started here, folks.

There was about a week in there where we thought our book was finished, when we suspected we had covered every available inch of our homes and loved ones with handknits.

But it doesn't work that way, this knitting stuff. Kay goes off bleaching denim yarn, Ann keeps fooling around with the Shetland wools, we keep seeing delicious things all over the wondrous land called Knitopia, and we discover a profound truth: It. Never. Ends.

It's not like we've run out of steam; we've simply run out of room. One of the first comments we received when we began our blog came from our dear pal Elisabeth Palladino, who said that Mason-Dixon Knitting was like "hanging out in the finished basement of your best friend." Eggzackly, we thought. The Internet is a rec room for everybody, and there's always more space on the busted-out corduroy sofa. Please stop by www.masondixonknitting.com to say hello, and to show everybody what you're working on. We can't wait to see.

ACKNOWLEDGMENTS

To say we needed a little help with this book is putting it mildly. When we turned to friends, even friends we knew only on the Internet, they pitched in and saved our bacon. We'd like to knit something for them all, and someday, we will.

We thank you. Thank you thank you!

★ To the readers of masondixonknitting.com: We salute you! Your goodwill, talent, and wicked sense of humor are an inspiration to us. It is a never-ending joy to hang out with you.

★ To Rick Shaver, Lee Melahn, and Emmy Shaver-Melahn, and Phyllis Howe and Richard Bradspies, who let us take over their beautiful homes for photography sessions.

★ To those who bravely volunteered to knit for us, and did it so quickly and perfectly: Maggie Bergmann, Wendy Brandes, Linda Greenebaum, Pamela Hubbard, Amelia Jones, Cheryl Klimaszewski, Heather Lee, Carolyn McGraw, Helen Meador, Mary Neal Meador, Benedetta Sarno, Joan Blum Shayne, Sissel Skjaerstadt, Robin Smith, Kathy Thompson, and Sarah Winsor.

★ To Thomas Holm, for the magnificent Shetland shawl of which we share joint custody.

★ To our models, some of whom were pressed into service on the spot: Carrie Bergmann, Joseph Bergmann, Maggie Bergmann, Paul Bergmann, Annie Bourque, Julia Case-Levine, Rose Xin Ye Hassel, Heather Lee, Indira Roth, and David Shayne.

★ To those who designed projects and those who inspired and encouraged our design efforts: Sarah Bradberry, Ann Hahn Buechner, Phyllis Howe, Brooks Jones, Polly Yee Outhwaite, Cristina Shiffman, Alison Green Will.

★ To those who lent us cool props: Kalani Craig of www.hapagirl.com, Plain Jane children's furnishings shop in New York City, Dorothy Reilly, and Laurie and Julia Weber.

★ To Kate Gilbert, for the line drawings that appeared, beautiful and perfect, all the way from Paris.

★ To Cara Davis Conomos, for the glamour shots.

★ To Jim Sherraden and the staff of Hatch Show Print, for turning us into country music singers, which has been our fantasy all along.

★ To Belinda Boaden, for her expertise and friendship.

★ To Michael Zibart, for endless wisdom.

★ To Angela Haglund, for her fine work with a box of old polo shirts and for cracking us up eight times a day.

★ To the visionaries who inspire us: Xenobia Bailey, Nicky Epstein, Kaffe Fassett, Debbie New and Barbara Walker, and the memory of Elizabeth Zimmermann, whose voice will always be in the ears of knitters looking for adventure.

★ To the Knitting Club of Revitz House, for all the afghan squares and fun.

★ To our families, who have suffered harsh privations in the name of handknits. We owe you each a sweater, but we know you'd prefer a Target gift card.

★ To photographers Steve Gross and Sue Daley, for the magnificent photography and for never batting an eye.

★ To the brilliant team at Potter Craft for showing us so much love, and for understanding what we are talking about when we talk about knitting: Jenny Frost, Lauren Shakely, Shawna Mullen, Marysarah Quinn, Lauren Monchik, Elizabeth Wright, Celia Johnson, Linnea Knollmueller, Amy Sly, and Chalkley Calderwood Pratt.

★ To Rosy Ngo, our wonderful editor whose talented eye has enhanced this book in so many ways.

★ To our agent Joy Tutela. How can we thank you, Joy? You saw this book from day one, before we really saw it ourselves.

THE QUEST FOR CHEAP YARN

Overcome sticker shock. Yarn can be rilly expensive. You're not going to save money by knitting your own clothes. You can buy a sweater at Target for what a skein of Colinette Point 5 costs. Don't get us wrong: we are grateful to the artisan yarn companies who are creating extraordinary, rare stuff. And it is downright unfriendly not to hang out at your local yarn store. Your core shopping should be in a place where you can pat your yarn before you buy it, and where you can ask a fellow customer, "Does this yarn make me look like I have consumption?"

We like a bargain, that's all. Here are our favorite ways to find great yarns for less.

www.eBay.com
Duh. Be sure to search for misspelled yarn names. Colinet instead of Colinette, Donagal for Donegal—for once, bad spelling is your friend.

www.texere.co.uk
Vast cones, huge drifts of yarn. If you're in the United States, you'll pay a lot for shipping because Texere is located in North Yorkshire, England. The prices are so good that you still come out ahead. If you're knitting rugs, bedspreads, or wall-to-wall carpet, you need this kind of heroic volume.

www.elann.com
Closeouts. Delicious, ever-changing closeouts.

www.colourway.co.uk
A shop in Wales that has fantastic sales of Rowan and Jaeger.

www.upcountry.co.uk
In the hometown of Rowan Yarns, Holmfirth, Yorkshire. Somehow it feels better to receive yarn that has breathed the same air as the folks at Rowan. You'll save money by buying direct from England, but do check the exchange rate first.

www.kangaroo.co.uk
Another British online source we love.

www.yarnxpress.com
Novelty yarn closeouts. Long on the bouclé and eyelash, but simple pleasures live here too.

www.elmore-pisgah.com
Peaches & Creme yarn at easy prices that will make you chuckle at your own cleverness.

BOOKS TO LEAD YOU TO GREAT HEIGHTS OF CREATIVE GENIUS

We hesitate to do this, because we are certain to omit some divine tract. That said, the following are books which have taught us a lot.

◉ *Knitting Without Tears*
BY ELIZABETH ZIMMERMANN

Her 1971 book is as fresh as paint. We still have a quibble with the title—the only tears we've ever wept while knitting have been those of abject joy at the realization that, for a short while, we are freed from making sippy cups of juice.

◉ *Elizabeth Zimmermann's Knitter's Almanac: Projects for Each Month of the Year.*
BY ELIZABETH ZIMMERMANN

When we grow up, we want to be Elizabeth Zimmermann. This book, which looks like it was written in 1912, has inspired online listservs of devoted knitters who are endlessly knitting the project of the month.

◉ While you're at it, pick up all the EZ you can find: *Knitting Around, Elizabeth Zimmermann's Knitting Workshop,* and *The Opinionated Knitter.*

◉ *The Principles of Knitting*
BY JUNE HEMMONS HIATT

There are any number of good all-purpose knitting references (*Vogue Knitting* is hard to beat), but this weirdly out-of-print book is a favorite. It's 571 pages of utterly straightforward instruction. Hiatt has answered every single knitting question I've ever had except "Why aren't I a faster knitter?" She is said to be revising the book, but we hold not our breath.

◉ *The Knitter's Handbook: A Comprehensive Guide to the Principles and Techniques of Handknitting*
BY MONTSE STANLEY

This is not a sleek book. At times it reads like a computer manual circa 1988 ("illustration 2.51a"?), but this alphabetical encyclopedia has a delicious mix of how-to (great line drawings) and wacky tidbits. (Peruvian knitters carry yarn over their necks, and often purl their colorwork in the round, inside out. Who knew?)

◉ *Rowan* magazine. Go ahead and start a collection. Knitting has never looked so good nor models so otherworldly. Rowan moves out of the craft book genre and straight into knitter's porn.

◉ *Loop-d-Loop: More than 40 Novel Designs for Knitters*
BY TEVA DURHAM

Two-and-a-half words for you: short-row Fair Isle. The word *novel* only begins to describe Durham's innovation and curiosity. Even if you never make her Cabled Riding Jacket, you will draw inspiration from this book.

◉ *Knitting for Anarchists*
BY ANNA ZILBOORG

Ah! A manifesto! Such a distinctive voice here, and so much to chew on. Zilboorg exhorts us to free ourselves from written patterns and "regain our illiteracy."

We like the way she admits to sloth and self-indulgence right there in the Acknowledgments. We're still faking industry and generosity.

◉ *The Knitter's Book of Finishing Techniques*
BY NANCIE M. WISEMAN

There cannot be too much written about finishing techniques. OK, maybe there can, but the cheerful tone and lovely design of this book makes it all look like such tidy fun that you'll decide to stick a zipper on everything you knit.

◉ *Designing Knitwear*
BY DEBORAH NEWTON

There are ghosts of the '80s in some of the designs here, but who cares? Newton takes you through the whole dodgy process of cooking up your own sweater, with a zillion options for every element. You can indulge your nostalgia for *Dynasty* while gleaning serious piles of information about the construction of handknits.

◉ *Knitting from the Top*
BY BARBARA G. WALKER

This is the book that will liberate you from patterns. Over twenty years old, and timeless.

◉ *A Treasury of Knitting Patterns,* four volumes.
BY BARBARA G. WALKER

Sure, anybody can use two or three Barbara Walkers. If you end up buying Volume 4, consider yourself a true, hardcore Walker fan.

◉ *Alice Starmore's Book of Fair Isle Knitting*
BY ALICE STARMORE

Any book by Alice Starmore is worthy of deep, long study. Some admire her elaborate, subversive Aran patterns.

They look perfectly traditional until you look closely and see the unusual way she uses familiar patterns. Her colorwork is what makes us crazy—she works in a palette of 143 shades of Shetland wool, so her Fair Isles are spectacular in their subtlety and sophistication. The trick, of course, is getting hold of Starmore's books. Many are out of print and cost hundreds of dollars. This is where inter-library loan can come in handy. Or high-end eBay investment. Or "borrowing."

The Knitter's Handy Book of Patterns: Basic Designs in Multiple Sizes and Gauges and The Knitter's Handy Book of Sweater Patterns
BY ANN BUDD

A godsend. These two volumes will get the most math-averse English major through the basics of sweater design. If you can circle a number, you can create your own pattern.

Unexpected Knitting
BY DEBBIE NEW

Don't expect to read this book on the subway home from the bookstore. Expect to read it for the rest of your life. Awe is the only possible reaction. Be bold, try some of New's techniques, and direct some of the awe toward yourself.

Kaffe Fassett's Pattern Library
BY KAFFE FASSETT

Start here to get the big picture of what Kaffe Fassett is all about: exuberant, over-the-top geometrics, fruits, flowers, and color, color, COLOR. These patterns can be adapted to whatever project you have in mind.

Once you've snacked on the Pattern Library, your Kaffe buffet can stretch as far as you like. He has been publishing books since the 1980s, exploring needle-point, patchwork, and even mosaic. All of it can inspire and enrich your knitting. *Kaffe's Classics: 25 Glorious Knitting Designs* is a greatest hits collection of sweaters. Particularly great if you like your sweaters coronation-worthy.

Knitting in Plain English, Sweater Design in Plain English
BY MAGGIE RIGHETTI

The thoughtful, no-nonsense advice in Maggie Righetti's books is the next best thing to sitting at the feet of a vastly experienced knitter. She shares the tricks of the trade, in plain English indeed.

The Seaton Collection: Exclusive Knitting Designs
BY JAMIE AND JESSI SEATON

In this 1989 book, Jamie and Jessi Seaton taught us that there is no rule against knitting a little Catullus into a cardigan. At times, these two make Kaffe Fassett's designs look a bit under-stated. We also suspect that they were the first to pair yellow short-shorts with intarsia sweaters, but we cannot be sure of that. Exhilarating designs that will embolden you.

Knitting on the Edge and Knitting Over the Edge
BY NICKY EPSTEIN

These books are beautifully pho-tographed stitch dictionaries and much more. Spend a little time

with them, and you will find fresh inspiration here. We also think the book's dedication to Madame DeFarge was long overdue in the knitting book genre.

The Knitting Experience, Book 1: The Knit Stitch, Book 2: The Purl Stitch, and Book 3: Color
BY SALLY MELVILLE

This series starts out as a basic how-to course, but there is so much for the experienced knitter to learn about tailor-ing and design. An invaluable source of knitterly techniques.

The Quilts of Gee's Bend
BY JOHN BEARDSLEY ET AL.

This book, which celebrates the stun-ning work of a community of Alabama quilters, may not technically be a knit-ting book, but we are here to tell you that you can knit from this book. And love it.

KNITTING TERMS AND ABBREVIATIONS

beg begin(ning)

BO bind off

CO cast on

cm centimeter(s)

cont continu(e)(ing)

dec decreas(e)(ing)

dpn(s) double-pointed needle(s)

foll follow(s)(ing)

g grams(s)

garter stitch Knit every row.

inc increase(e)(ing)

kfb Knit into front and back of stitch.

k knit

k2tog Knit 2 stitches together.

m meter(s)

M1 Make one stitch.

mm millimeter(s)

oz ounce(s)

pat(s) pattern(s)

p purl

psso pass slip stitch(es) over

rem remain(s)(ing)

rep repeat

RS right side(s)

rnd(s) round(s)

SKP Slip 1, knit 1, pass slip stitch over knit 1. One stitch has been descreased

sl slip—An unworked stitch made by passing a stitch from the left-hand needle to the right-hand needle as if to purl.

sl st slip stitch

SSK Slip, slip, knit—Slip next 2 stitches knitwise, one at a time, to right-hand needle. Insert tip of left-hand needle into fronts of these stitches from left to right. Knit them together. One stitch has been decreased.

st(s) stitch(es)

St st Stockinette stitch—Knit right-side rows, purl wrong-side rows.

tbl through back loop(s)

tog together

WS wrong side(s)

yf yarn forward

yb yarn back

yd yard(s)

yo yarn over—Make a new stitch by wrapping the yarn over the right-hand needle. (UK:yfwd, yon, yrn)

[ ] = Repeat directions inside brackets as many times as indicated.

INDEX OF PROJECTS

INDEX

YARNS WE LOVE TO KNIT

We got our yarn the old-fashioned way: we went to a local yarn store, we looked, we touched, we drooled, and eventually we handed over our credit cards. Here is a handy list of the manufacturers of the yarns specified in our patterns. The websites give up-to-date information on shops and online sellers.

Baabajoes Wool Company
www.baabajoeswool.com

Brown Sheep Company, Inc.
http://brownsheep.com

Cascade Yarns
http://cascadeyarns.com

Classic Elite Yarns
www.classiceliteyarns.com

Coats & Clark
www.coatsandclark.com

Crystal Palace Yarns
www.crystalpalaceyarns.com

Elmore-Pisgah, Inc.
www.elmore-pisgah.com

Elsebeth Lavold
www.knittingfever.com

Great Adirondack
www.personalthreads.com

Harrisville Designs
www.harrisville.com

Lang Yarns
www.langyarns.ch/en

Louet Sales
www.louet.com

Noro Yarns
www.knittingfever.com

Rowan
www.knitrowan.com

Tahki Yarns/Tahki Stacy Charles, Inc.
www.tahkistacycharles.com

Remember: No project is too ambitious
if you crave the result enough.